Freedom from Stress

Freedom from Stress

A Holistic Approach

Phil Nuernberger, Ph.D.

Foreword by Barbara B. Brown, Ph.D.

Himalayan International Institute
of Yoga Science and Philosophy
Publishers

The quotation by T. S. Eliot is from "Little Gidding" in *Four Quartets* and is reprinted by permission of Harcourt Brace Jovanovich, Inc.; copyright 1943 by T. S. Eliot; copyright 1971 by Esme Valerie Eliot. The Himalayan Institute has granted permission to quote from the following works: Rudolph Ballentine, M.D., *Diet and Nutrition*, copyright 1978; Rudolph Ballentine, M.D., ed., *Joints and Glands Exercises*, copyright 1977; Samskrti and Veda, *Hatha Yoga Manual I*, copyright 1977; Swami Rama and Swami Ajaya, *Emotion to Enlightenment*, copyright 1976. In addition, the Himalayan Institute has granted permission to reproduce drawings from Usharbudh Arya, *Philosophy of Hatha Yoga*, copyright 1977, and Swami Rama et al., *Science of Breath*, copyright 1979.

Library of Congress Catalog Card Number: 80-80542

ISBN 0-89389-064-2
ISBN 0-89389-071-5 pbk

Acknowledgements

There are many people involved in producing a book, and the author wishes to express his gratitude to the following: John Clarke, M.D. for his invaluable contributions to the development of this work; John Harvey, Ph.D., for his technical help; Alan Hymes, M.D., and Richard Leifer, Ph.D., for their data; Anne Craig and Arpita for their editorial patience and skill; and Theresa O'Brien, Randy Padorr-Black and Janet Zima for their typesetting, design and illustrations.

Whatever merit this book has, however, is due to the guidance of my teacher, Sri Swami Rama. Without him it could not have been written. Thanks are also due to my parents who were my first teachers. Finally, special thoughts are given to my lovely wife who was a constant support for my efforts and provided generous encouragement—and to my daughter for patiently (mostly) waiting for her playmate.

Foreword

There are two marks of those special life scientists who always seem to be able to expand the perimeters of knowledge and our understanding of the connectedness of life: they neither float lightly on the scientific currents nor do they sail casually on the intellectual seas. They are the Magellans of life science research who mix visions of new horizons with the solid substance of scholarship, detect obscure marker buoys, and steer a steady course through unknown waters of science.

Dr. Nuernberger's book, *Freedom from Stress*, describes a journey of exploration through the territory of stress that few realize is still uncharted. Most explorers claiming acquaintance with stress know it only through the emotional and physical debris it tosses on their clinical shores or from simulations they contrive in laboratories, and they have not searched for nor seen the lodestars marking the passageways from stress to distress and back again to health.

The beauty of this book has many dimensions: coherence, clarity, rationality, thoughtfulness, and practicality. It not merely guides the traveler through the murky depths of stress, it does so with ease and clarity flowing so smoothly it seems almost like a familiar journey. But it is not.

It is, instead, a journey through the inner byways of the workaday functioning of mind and body, with the focus always on how such ordinary, habitual processes operate between the circumstances of stress and the visceral, muscle, or emotionally painful consequences of stress. Not before in medical or psychological literature have the circumstances of stress, the feelings they engender, and the debilitating imprint they leave on emotions and physiological functions been described so unpretentiously and with such relevance to the events and feelings of everyday life. It becomes clear, too, how pervasive and threatening stress is to productive, fulfilling ways of being. The author underscores the growing hazards of stress to human welfare in a convincing examination of the failures of conventional ways for dealing with stress and the high costs of these failures that, as he points out, deal with relief of symptoms and do not treat causes. As Dr. Nuernberger leads us through the wasting stretches of stress in all avenues of life, and as he reveals the inner devitalizing effects of stress, the ineffective ways we deal with stress and the extravagence of our inefficiencies, we realize that stress has seized a unique place in the compendium of human ailments and afflictions.

One task the author faced at the outset was the clearing away of a widespread confusion and misunderstanding about the nature of stress—vague, often inappropriate notions shaped from models designed to account only for the physical consequences of stress. These foggy notions have also led to an unprecedented muddle of terminology. Dr. Nuernberger documents the errors of prevailing ideas about stress, pointing out clearly contradictory evidence, then mending the arguments and clarifying terms by patient analysis of the events of stress as they are and can be observed objectively. It is just this patience and clarity—by which one is taken through the operations of the vast networks linking the vital systems of the human organism that achieve the balance and harmony of function required for fruitful, fulfilling life—that allows intimate understanding of the nature of stress. And understanding the nature of balanced physiological functioning is, in fact, one key to understanding stress.

But this, of course, is only one part of the story. By this time, the author has made you realize that stress demons are born only out of the life within. Then, with his skills for literally seeing inside the functioning brain and body, Dr. Nuernberger takes you inside the mind, as a hand-holding guide who lets you see and feel the events of mind that can go astray and pull the body with it. It is, surprisingly, the very ordinariness of thought—our common, everyday reactions to people and events—that nonetheless exert extraordinary effects on feelings and the behavior of the body. This is a lucid, involving narrative account of how thoughts generate feelings and feelings generate disturbing emotions and physical distress.

Then comes the second key to understanding stress: the understanding that we lack awareness of our habits—our mental, emotional, and body habits—that are hidden within the unconscious and are the real source of stress. And now that the author has lifted the threefold guises of behavior and shown the processes of habit and of mind-body balance, he leads us on to new ways for self-training to become aware of the habit demons of stress and to mastery over their interferences in functioning wholly, in harmony, and without stress.

The explanations of how to achieve self-awareness are, again, most skillful. There are fascinating glimpses into how to detect one's mind, emotion, and body habits, clues about food and exercise habits, and unusually enlightening explanations of the physiology of breathing, breathing habits, the whys and hows of breathing exercises, and finally, a superbly clear, step-by-step explanation of the practice and merits of meditation. The extraordinary coherence of the book culminates with its by now obvious conclusions, the conclusions that awareness of the inner being not merely smothers and overrides stress, but transforms personality and leads to the ultimate freedom, the freedom to know and to choose our responses in life.

One thing more should be said. I may seem unusually enthusiastic in this foreword, enthusiastic that someone has, at last, attempted unraveling the perplexing riddles of stress and done such an admirable job, and there is a special reason for this. I have been a casual follower of Phil Nuernberger's research activities for some time, but our occasional discussions have tended to center on biofeedback. So I was startled (although I shouldn't have been) to learn that he had not only formulated a completely new perspective of stress and stress management, but also that this new perspective shared features of a concept I had been developing in my corner of the world. There are points of disagreement, to be sure, but the gist of the two views is similar enough for each of us to feel reinforced and confirmed. I tend to emphasize the mechanisms of the intellect and how its operations affect the psyche, while Dr. Nuernberger provides an intimate account of the subtle interplay among nerves, vital organs, hormones, muscles, and the center of awareness. We have both, however, from our different starting points arrived at quite similar conclusions about how the unobserving mind itself breeds stress and how self-observations and awareness yield an interior knowledge that matures to a self-mastery stress cannot penetrate. My delight with *Freedom from Stress* springs from its lucid descriptions of the obscure and subtle operations of the mind (and their interface with the mind's own biological substrate) to both cause and cure stress and from its prescriptions for recognizing the inner resources for fulfilling each human potential. *Freedom from Stress* is, in a large sense, a guide to inner transformations.

I have not one doubt but that every reader of *Freedom from Stress* will share my joy over its unique blend of science and common sense, of concept and practical exercise, of physiology and psychology, and explanations that transcend apparent differences between East and West views of mind and body and brain.

Barbara B. Brown, Ph.D.

Contents

Introduction

We are a perpetually anxious species. We are constantly creating stress by not having control over our environment. A human being is the architect of his own destiny, but we have allowed fear, loneliness and despair to disturb us through the ages. Ancient myths describe great struggles; the Vedas are full of intense yearning, and Genesis tells of the fall from grace to misery. Christ in the Sermon on the Mount talks about perfection, and Christianity maintains that a human being has to be free from imperfections in order to attain the ultimate reality. Buddha established his philosophy on the premise that life is suffering, and the Yoga Sutras are directed to those who seek liberation from the bonds of human sorrow, strain and stress.

Even in these early times, when life seems to have been simpler than it is now, people were born in pain, separated from what they loved and subject to sickness, old age and death. This is still true, for pleasure, wealth, fame and power have never been able to dispel the basic ignorance which is at the core of human existence. In modern times religion, philosophy, and psychology have attempted to explain and ease our condition. They have also tried to identify that "something more" which we either believe in blindly or desperately hope for. But the joy, wisdom and sense of being complete of which we dream continues to escape us. Our attempts to find it are thwarted by our ignorance, by our narrow self-concept, and by the craving for personal happiness which motivates us.

This situation has been a burden to man since the beginning of human consciousness, and now it seems to be even more intense. The rapid pace and complex demands of modern life add to the weight of that which is already on his shoulders. Existentialism reflects this state with its talk of nothingness. It is also reflected in our spirit by a pervasive sense of emptiness and yearning; it is reflected in our mind by what is called "free floating anxiety" as well as by deep-seated depression.

In our bodies, our state of mind is reflected in various aches and pains as well as in a number of stress-related diseases such as hypertension and ulcers. Strokes, cancer, heart disease and mental illness are also prevalent—and also stress-related. In fact, most diseases are now linked to the state of sustained stress in which most of us live. This stems directly from our frustrations, worries and despondency, for as we race faster and faster for rewards that mean less and less, we still get nowhere—and our stress grows. Shakespeare might have been speaking of the age we live in when he said, "everyone can master grief but he who has it."

In the past, wise teachers developed therapeutic and pragmatic systems (such as those found in Christianity, Buddhism and the science of yoga) in order to free us from suffering. Now, with an epidemic of stress-related complaints spreading through our society, modern science has also joined these efforts, and many stress-reduction techniques have recently emerged. This is essential to our needs since many modern people, finding it difficult to understand or accept some of the ancient methods for dealing with their problems, will turn to the scientists for help.

Scientific research, however, though sophisticated, is aimed only at the physical level, while stress is a condition of the mind and reflects its symptom in the body. Thus, seeking solutions from the medical and psychological professions can be confusing, for experts in these fields often do not agree with one another.

It is not clear, for example, whether stress is a function of personality variables, of intrinsic physiological responses to environmental intrusions, or of learned cognitive/behavioral patterns. Friedman and Rosen (1974) correlate high degrees of stress with a pattern of personality characteristics they label Type A (what they call the Type B personality pattern demonstrates low levels of stress). Pelletier (1977) also postulates that certain personality traits are destructive to health because they increase stress. Many other studies have suggested interesting correlations between personality traits and stress-related diseases, but it remains difficult to demonstrate a clear causal link here. Averill, Olbrich and Lazarus (1972) caution that the majority of reported personality correlates may not hold up under replication.

Other researchers point toward a straightforward, innate physiological response (on the part of the organism to environmental stimuli) as the source of stress. Kobasa (1976), for instance, has devised a checklist of stressful life situations which may lead to illness by overtaxing the body's ability to deal with prolonged anxiety. Selye (1956) describes a fight-or-flight response on the part of the nervous system when threat is perceived, and Benson (1976) contrasts this with what he terms the relaxation response. Diet is also found to be closely involved with stress, and doctors prescribe nutritional elements (Williams, 1971) for decreasing the levels of stress in the organism. It is also quite common for doctors to prescribe mood-altering drugs to patients who complain of anxiety or depression and to treat the symptoms of psychosomatic complaints such as headaches, with medications.

A third group of researchers feel that stress affects all personality types and is more than just a physiological reflex, citing its major cause as behavioral and cognitive habits dealing with conditioning and perceptual processes. Davidson and Schwartz (1976) emphasize that at least three components are active in all stress reactions—somatic, cognitive and attentional—and that interventions should be undertaken in relation to the ways in which the individual experiences stress. In addition, many therapists see patterns of obsessive, negative thinking as learned behaviors (or habits) which can either create stress or be redesigned to foster a more rational, balanced, less stress-producing outlook on life. Thus a number of body/mind therapies such as Rolfing, the Alexander technique, bioenergetics and others have become very popular of late, for they deal directly with the physical/mental/emotional symptoms of stress.

In spite of a wide range of theories and therapies for treating stress, however, stress-related diseases are increasing. What is more, there has been no comprehensive or definitive text to date in which the average person could find a clear explanation of the source, process and effects of stress, or learn of the various scientifically-tested new techniques (as well as the time-tested traditional methods) for treating it. The problems caused by stress therefore remain among the most pressing of our times; they affect each of us personally as well as influence the course of society as a whole.

In *Freedom from Stress*, Dr. Nuernberger gives us the information and procedures that are so urgently needed. Trained in both ancient and modern therapeutic interventions, the author offers us, in lucid language, a comprehensive system of the theoretical and applied knowledge which both professional and layman can use to eliminate stress.

Dr. Nuernberger defines prolonged stress as a constant imbalance in the involuntary nervous system; he then describes how this is brought about and how it affects the person as a whole and explains the function of the physiological and psychological components involved. The rationale and procedures for a stress-reduction program are then given, in which he uses a holistic approach directed toward every aspect of the human being: body, breath and mind. It clarifies and selectively applies the current theories of Western practitioners and combines them with practices derived from traditional Eastern disciplines. The comprehensive self-training program he describes thus enables one to understand how to deal with stress and eventually eliminate it. This program includes exercises in stretching, relaxation and breathing, and it explains how diet and lifestyle, thoughts and emotions can contribute to levels of anxiety. He focuses on awareness, attitudes and, primarily, meditation as important elements in learning to live free from stress.

An experienced counseling psychologist and student of yoga, Dr. Nuernberger is well qualified to write about the ancient and modern techniques for relieving stress, and in this book he gives us a clear, practical and comprehensive synthesis of procedures for doing so. With this information one can learn to be his own therapist and to treat his own anxieties. A self-training program such as the one described in this book is the most effective means for dealing with stress because it places responsibility with the individual himself. As the Upanishads tell us, "Since it is the self by which we suffer, so it is the self by which we will find relief."

When one learns to understand that the nucleus of stress resides in the inner chamber of his own being, he learns to organize his internal states. He is thus able to create a joyous, stress-free and tranquil atmosphere around himself. A human being can do this. He can learn to live a stress-free life. Such a person becomes a responsible citizen and contributes significantly to creative ways of living and being—here and now. He knows how to live in the world and yet remain above it.

Swami Rama
August 11, 1980

Stress
Part One

Stress–The Threat from Within

Every era in history has been characterized by some debilitating disease. In the Western cultures, for instance, there were the plagues of the Middle Ages, the consumption of the Romantic period, and the ravages of polio and pneumonia in the early 1900's. For the most part, these diseases were eliminated when the environmental conditions were improved or when the germs or viruses were destroyed through drugs.

In modern society, we too have a characteristic disease, but one that is not so easy to eliminate. It underlies such diverse conditions as psychosomatic disease, heart disease and chemical dependency, and it is a major contributor to disturbances in one's emotional, social and family life. It inhibits creativity and personal effectiveness, and it is present in the sense of general dissatisfaction that is so obvious in our day-to-day lives. The name of this condition is stress, and it has been called by medical researchers at Cornell University

Medical College "the most debilitating medical and social problem in the U.S. today."

It is hard to imagine how a single cause can contribute to such a variety of disorders until one realizes that it is the very fabric of our lives that is involved. Stress is uniquely different from what we normally think of as a disease. It has no biological structure such as a germ or virus, nor does it lurk in dank sewers or contaminated water. Rather, it is the result of how our mind and body function and interact. It is psychosomatic in the true sense of the word—*psyche* meaning "mind" and *soma* meaning "body." It is the consequence of how we regulate, or to put it more appropriately, how we do not regulate, the mental and physical functioning of our being. In a few short words, stress is the result of the way we have consciously or unconsciously chosen to live.

It is the "dis-ease" created by the abuse we give our minds and bodies, and it leads to an incredible variety of symptoms. They may be as innocuous as a temper tantrum or as destructive as a heart attack. Stress may show itself in alcoholism or in depression. It leads to sleeplessness and to the common cold. Its symptoms are many, while its cause often goes unrecognized and untreated.

Stress is more than being "up-tight" occasionally, or having a bad day. It is a recurring imbalance resulting in the daily wear-and-tear on the body that leads to dysfunction and debilitation. It comes in different guises. Emotional stress (or mental stress) is the stress generated by our personality as we interact with our environment on a day-to-day basis (this is sometimes referred to as social stress). Digestive stress is the stress we get from poor eating habits. Environmental stress is created by such factors as smog, noise and air pollution. The reason stress is harmful is because we are un-consciously creating it, and we become accustomed to sustaining it. Consequently we come to accept stress as a "normal" part of everyday life. In fact, we have even come to believe that some stress is good for us—this is a misperception which is akin to saying, "Some headaches are good for us." In truth, however, it is the frequently recurring stress result-ing in a constant level of unrelieved stress—stress that stems from our inner habits of being whether we are aware of it or not—that leads to disease.

We do a variety of things to cope with this problem, much of which, however, is only palliative. For instance, medical treatment is focused upon the symptoms but does little for the underlying condition or cause. On our own we smoke, drink, take aspirins and sleeping tablets, have massages, watch T.V., go on vacations and even practice relaxation techniques—with precious little success in allevi-ating the actual stress. And the frequency and variety of its symptoms are on the increase.

One of the reasons for this is that stress is not a "thing" such as a germ, or virus, or bad water. It cannot be put on a slide and under a microscope, or bottled, or separated into categories and counted. Our past success in controlling disease has been because we could do these things, and this success has blinded us to the real nature of the problem of stress. We still focus our attention outward in a futile attempt to "come to grips" with whatever it is out there that is a killer. In doing so, in looking for the causes externally, we have not paid attention to the source of stress—the way we as individuals think, feel and act.

This dependence on past models of health has also led

to the confusion between "good stress" and "bad stress," for these models fail to recognize the role of awareness and will as well as the difference between directed tension and undirected tension. In short, we have failed to understand the psychosomatic nature of stress. We do benefit from exercising, voluntarily and with full awareness, utilizing both arousal and relaxation. The consequences of this are increased health, increased capacity and increased effectiveness. But this is because we have been able to maintain a balance. *Stress in itself is always harmful. No one has ever benefited from stress.*

It is possible to achieve optimal, balanced and, thus, stress-free, living, and there is an approach to health care that shows us how we can do this. It is called holistic health, and it is based on the realization that everyone is, in the last analysis, responsible for his own health rather than having to depend upon the doctor or the drug or the drink. Holistic health provides the framework necessary to understand and really conquer stress. Utilizing such tools as biofeedback and meditation, for instance, holistic health gives us a functional approach to conquering stress that is based on training rather than therapy—prevention rather than cure. Its focus is the entire person—body, mind and spirit, and this is exactly what is needed to deal with psychosomatic disease. Interestingly enough, this modern approach has its roots in yoga science, one of the oldest disciplines known to man.

By understanding the source of stress, then, our own selves, we can begin to alter and conquer it. For if we are the source of our own disease, we can also be its cure. In the following chapters we will explore stress in all its forms, employing a holistic perspective that can provide the necessary understanding and tools by which we can become free from it. This is very possible. We have the resources to do it. We do not have to sustain stress. But first we should take a closer look at just how destructive stress is in our society.

Psychosomatic Disease

There is general agreement that a high percentage (perhaps as high as seventy to eighty per cent) of our diseases are psychosomatic and that their primary causes are our thoughts, attitudes and beliefs. This is not to say that the symptoms of disease (such as pain from an ulcer or a headache) are imaginary; they are certainly real enough, and real physiological changes do occur. What psychosomatic means is that the major source of the disease lies in one's emotional/mental/perceptual and behavioral habits. In other words, the way that we have been conditioned to react to our environment has resulted in internal physiological changes which either evolve into disease or allow disease states to exist.

It is these subtle, conditioned habits which result in physiological damage. As Dr. Barbara Brown points out in *Stress and the Art of Biofeedback*, what disease occurs, and which internal process is involved, is the consequence of a very complex interaction of psychological, constitutional or genetic and environmental factors. The pattern will be unique for each individual. For example, one person may suppress anger and eventually develop the mental dysfunction of depression; another may suppress anger and eventually develop migraine headaches. But even though the development of the specific psychosomatic disease is unique to each individual, the underlying principles are the same. Emotional stress leads to physiological stress—and this results in an eventual breakdown (disease) of the target organ system.

A classic example of how this works can be found in the case of the ever-popular ulcer. The personality characteristics typically associated with ulcers are a high degree of competitiveness, a tendency to exaggerate worries, difficulty in expressing feelings of anger and fear openly, and poor dietary and eating habits (such as eating when one is tense and eating too fast). These traits result in an overly acidic condition in the gastro-intestinal tract. Poor eating habits further aggravate the internal condition (interfering with proper digestion), and the overly-acidic internal environment "eats away" at the lining of the stomach wall, or duodenum, thus creating an ulcer. This, besides being extremely painful, can lead to such dangerous complications as internal bleeding. The ulcer could have been prevented had we attended to the early symptoms.

By paying careful attention to personal history, one can nearly always trace the origins of psychosomatic disease back to patterns of emotional pressures. Dr. Katil Udupa, an internationally recognized neurosurgeon, reports that psychosomatic diseases appear to progress through four distinct phases:

Psychic Phase: This phase is marked by mild but persistent psychological and behavioral symptoms of stress, such as irritability, disturbed sleep or any of the symptoms given in Table 2 on pages 26-27.

Psychosomatic Phase: If the stress continues there is an increase in symptoms, along with the beginnings of generalized physiological symptoms such as occasional hypertension and tremors.

Somatic Phase: This phase is marked by increased function of the organs, particularly the target, or involved organ. At this stage one begins to identify the beginnings of a disease state.

Organic Phase: This phase is marked by the full involvement of a so-called disease state, with physiological changes such as an ulcerated stomach or chronic hypertension becoming manifest.

Often, however, the early stages of the disease process are overlooked and the final stage is seen as an entity unto itself, having little relationship to one's living habits and patterns.

There are many examples of psychosomatic diseases which are directly related to stress. They include common colds, ulcers, headaches, many kinds of back pains, chest pains, spastic colons, constipation and diarrhea. The list is almost endless. We don't know why one organ system is affected by stress and not another. Certainly, genetic factors, diet and conditioned learning are all involved, but the key lies in one's mental structures. In other words, what is increasingly clear is that stress is at the root of all psychosomatic disease regardless of the organ system involved.

Heart Disease: The Popular Way to Die

Research is also beginning to reveal a direct relationship

between stress and CVD, and statements such as the following made at the National Conference on Emotional Stress and Heart Disease are becoming commonplace at national psychological and medical conferences. Emotional stress is "associated with significant blood pressure changes in both normotensive and hypertensive man. The data is quite firm on this point," and, "Much persuasive evidence has been developed with regard to the potential for emotional stress to represent a significant factor in coronary heart disease and sudden death. Uniformly, it was concluded that emotional stress is, indeed, a major factor in the pathogenesis of coronary heart disease." According to the data collected, we find that strokes and heart disease are the greatest killers, and stress is often the basis of these diseases.

Much of the pioneering work in this area has been done by Drs. Meyer Friedman and Ray Rosenman. In *Type A Behavior and Your Heart*, they point out that there is a certain personality type (the Type A personality) that is very prone to CVD. Another personality type (the Type B personality) does not usually develop CVD. Table 1 below lists the kinds of behavioral patterns which are typical of both types. Type A personalities are under almost constant pressure to perform. They are hurried, impatient and often hostile. Type A personalities always seem to be short of time, but they don't recognize that they have overcrowded themselves. On the other hand, the Type B personality appears to be relaxed and free from the urgencies of time. He doesn't harbor much anger and he generally has the ability to enjoy his work or play. Statistically, he is free from CVD. In spite of what one might think, however, Type A personalities do not accomplish more than Type B's. They only exert more

TABLE 1
CHARACTERISTIC BEHAVIOR PATTERNS
OF TYPE A AND TYPE B PERSONALITIES

Type A Behaviors:

- Hurried speech.
- Constant, rapid movement/eating.
- Open impatience with the rate at which things occur and how others operate; chronic sense of time urgency.
- Thinking and performing several things at once.
- An active attempt to dominate the conversation, to determine the topics, and to remain pre-occupied with one's own thoughts when others are talking.
- Vague guilty feelings during periods of relaxation, when doing nothing.
- Overconcern with getting things worth having—no time to become the things worth being.
- No compassion for other Type A's.
- Characteristic nervous gestures—tics, clench fist and jaw, pound on table, grind teeth.

Type B Behaviors:

- Complete freedom from all the Type A traits.
- No sense of time urgency.
- No free-floating hostility.
- No felt need to display or discuss one's achievements and accomplishments unless the situation demands it.
- A belief that play exists for fun and relaxation, not to exhibit superiority.
- An ability to relax without guilt and to work without agitation.

effort in order to do the same amount of work that Type B's accomplish in a much more relaxed way.

There is another personality type not included in *Type A Behavior and Your Heart* that we may call Type C, the coping personality. These are the ones who sustain considerable stress but who have learned to cope with it; whether or not they are bothered with CVD depends on how well they have learned to do this. Many of us are in this category, for nearly all of us share some of the characteristics of the Type A personality—and the more involved with them we are, the more involved we are with stress.

The busy executive is often the classic example of the Type A personality. In fact, one could reasonably describe the typical executive as follows:

One who is engaged in a ceaseless struggle to obtain certain optimum conditions, rewards or results in a limited time and often against opposition (from competitors, structural conditions, or even colleagues).

One who is often under pressure to achieve more in less time (to become more efficient).

One who accepts challenges and prefers to overcome them rather than retreat.

One who usually exhibits enhanced personality traits of aggressiveness, ambitiousness and the competitive drive.

One who is work-oriented.

One who likes to play hard, who may be explosive in speech and who is often referred to as intense.

But actually, it does not matter whether one is an executive or plumber, a carpenter or college student. It is not the job, but the attitudes and behavior that one brings to it, that determine whether or not one is a Type A personality —and thus prone to CVD.

What is more, CVD is not a respecter of sex. Women have been notoriously free from it until recently, but as they have become accepted into executive and other male-dominated positions that seem to require certain Type A behaviors and attitudes, there has been a corresponding increase in CVD in their ranks. In fact, physicians such as Dr. Alan Hymes, a thoracic surgeon, report that women whose lifestyles have been altered to fit executive careers have shown up to a two-thousand percent increase in coronary problems. In other words, heart disease is not discriminatory; it is an equal-opportunity disease for anyone who develops the required life style.

The most pervasive cardiovascular disease is high blood pressure, or hypertension, and it is especially dangerous because ordinarily there are no warnings or symptoms unless one has his blood pressure checked periodically. Hypertension often leads to tragic consequences—and the higher the blood pressure, the higher the risk of developing hardening of the arteries—and this leads to the deadly problems of heart attacks and strokes.

As Dr. Herbert Benson, author of *The Relaxation Response*, points out, the mechanical, or physiological, causes for hypertension are few. A constricted artery to the kidney is the cause of about two to five percent of high blood pressure problems. Other physical causes can be pregnancy, tumors of the brain or adrenal glands, or some malfunction of the thyroid gland. However, ninety to ninety-five percent of all cases of hypertension are known as "essential hypertension." That is, there is no known physiological reason for it. The chief suspect is stress, but in spite of the statistics, very little is known about it within traditional medical circles. Even less is known about eliminating it.

Many factors are involved in CVD including diet, smoking, family history, drinking habits and exercise, but stress underlies most of them. Chart 1 is a coronary factors profile developed by Richard Leifer, Ph.D., of the University of Massachusetts, for use in stress management seminars. Take a moment and outline your profile. Make a dot in the center of each column as to whether you are in the High, Moderate or Low Risk category. Then connect the dots.

Don't be easy on yourself, and don't give yourself the benefit of the doubt. The profile can be very helpful if you are honest with your appraisal, for it can point out where you have weaknesses that can lead to the development of cardiovascular disease. Remember that in order to prevent CVD, the first step is to become aware of the stress-related habits and behavior that can lead to it. You will notice that every category, with the exception of Family History, is under your control. That is, there are intelligent choices you can make if you want to prevent CVD.

The Tension Headache Syndrome

There are also intelligent choices you can make if you

CHART 1
FACTORS INVOLVED IN CORONARY HEART DISEASE

Level of Risk	Job Situation	Life Changes	Personality Type	Diet	Blood Cholesteral	Family History of Stress Related Diseases	Smoking	Weight	Physical Activity	Salt Intake	Blood Pressure	Drinking Habits
High Risk	Occasionally or regularly take tranquilizers, feel tense or rushed more than half of the day.	A great number of changes in the past 12 months	A	At or above U.S. average of 24 times per week for meat, cheese or whole milk	201 - 220 or above	Two or more blood relatives	20 or more per day (one pack)	More than 20 pounds over-weight	Exercise rarely, normal walking, less than 2 - 2½ miles per day	Above average use of salt; frequent use of salty foods	Above 140 systolic and/or above 90 diastolic	Heavy
Moderate Risk	Feel tense about 2-3 times a day or frequent anger	A moderate number in the past 12 months	C	Mostly meat, eggs, cheese (12 times per week) non-fat milk only	165 - 200	One relative	Up to 20 per day	Up to 20 pounds over-weight	Vigorous exercise once or twice a week or irregular exercise or walk-ing	Salt in cooking— some to frequent use of salt at table	115 - 140 systolic 80 - 90 diastolic	Moderate
Low Risk	Feel contented and un-hurried most days	Few changes in the past 12 months	B	At least 4 meat-less days per week, lean meat only, no whole milk products, egg yolk infre-quently	Less than 165	No family history of heart disease, strokes, or ulcers	None	Up to 5 pounds over-weight	Vigorous exercise at least 3/week, 20 min. each, or brisk walking 3/week 30 min. each	No use of salt at table Spare use of high salt foods	Less than 115 systolic; less than 80 diastolic	None to Mild

Adapted for use in Stress Management Seminars by Richard Leifer, Ph.D.

want to prevent tension headaches, for they are a classic example of how psychosomatic disease is related to stress as it manifests in chronic muscle tension. In other words, suppose that for some reason the muscles of your neck and shoulders remain tense. This creates tremendous pressure on the skull, and this will often lead to a tension headache. The headache, however is only the consequence of whatever caused the muscle tension in the first place; the headache is a symptom of the problem, not the problem itself. Other favorite targets of tension are the masseter muscles in the jaws, for often those who feel that they must not openly express anger clench their jaw muscles in an unconscious attempt to cover it. This too may result in a tension headache. The direct cause of the headache is muscle tension; the underlying cause is stress.

One of the characteristics of chronic muscle tension is that often one becomes aware of the tension only after it has reached the stage of pain. Long before this, however, the musculature has developed the habit of being clenched, or tightened, and once this has happened the muscle grouping will tend to repeat the habit until it is trained to do otherwise. By now, however, the habit has worked its way into our unconscious. For instance, those who habitually clench their jaw muscles will find that they do so even when there is no apparent reason for it.

If you will pause and reflect a moment, you can become aware of certain areas of muscle tension in your own body. Check your shoulders to see if they are slightly raised. Is your brow a little bit furrowed? Do you talk with your teeth clenched together? Do you grind your teeth at night? These are just a few of the more common symptoms of chronic muscle tension that can lead to headache.

Another whole symptom complex related to muscle tension is back pain, such as that which is often felt in the lumbar-sacral region. Instead of doing proper exercises which stretch the muscles and loosen the pressure on the spine, however, and instead of doing relaxation exercises which relieve the tension, we spend all day complaining of lower back pain. Then we run to the chiropractor or orthopoedic surgeon to relieve the conditions we have ourselves created by the unconscious play of emotions in our mind—which leads to stress—which leads to muscle tension—which leads to pain and disease.

Migraine headaches are much more complex than tension headaches, for they involve several internal systems of the body simultaneously. Often the reaction of the vascular system to stress, they are extremely painful and are frequently accompanied by visual patterns and nausea as well as muscular tension. In women, particularly, the hormonal system may also be involved.

Another common headache pattern is the severe tension/migraine headache which occurs only on weekends. This is a particular pain reaction to stress that affects corporation executives particularly—hence the name, "executive's headache." Those so afflicted simply do not have time to be sick during the week, so they allow the pain to manifest only on the weekends. What is really happening, however, is that the unconscious becomes more active at this time because the executive is more relaxed. Consequently, the symptoms emerge. Those involved do not always understand this process clearly, of course, but the pattern of pain is very consistent.

Thus, pain from chronic structural tension can be as simple and direct as muscle tension headaches, or it can be extremely complex as are migraine headaches. No matter what kind of pain it is, however, as Dr. Brown points out, relieving the tension materially assists in recovering from the disease.

Drug Abuse—Let's Have a Drink and Relax

The pervasive drug problem we have in this country is also directly related to stress. The most obvious example, of course, is alcohol—one of the most costly drugs we ingest, both financially and socially. Conservative estimates place five percent of the work force in the alcoholic category, and another five percent are labeled, "problem drinkers." A report to the National Institute on Alcohol Abuse and Alcoholism cites a 13 billion dollar expenditure for alcohol-related health and medical problems, and 20 billion dollars for lost production costs that are directly related to alcohol. Indirect cost estimates run as high as 45 billion dollars. So this is a fairly expensive habit. In addition, there is no way to compute the personal agony involved in alcoholism, nor do the figures truly reflect the loss of creative effectiveness within a corporate structure—the subtle changes in one's ability to think clearly and creatively—that come about through alcoholism.

Many people attempt to cope with their stress by drinking. The temporary "high" numbs painful emotions and seems to ease pressure—and this becomes a regular escape for them. But even though alcohol does create a short suppression of the sympathetic nervous system (and subsequent muscular and mental relaxation), these benefits turn out to be short-lived—and one is caught in a destructive cycle of drinking which creates more stress than existed previously. As one begins to depend on a few drinks to unwind and forget about the problems of the day, the pattern eventually becomes habitual, and an emotional and physical addiction creeps up on one before he realizes it. Then more and more alcohol is needed to attain the same effect.

Because of alcohol, one's perceptive and reasoning capacities are distorted and interpersonal relationships are seriously jeopardized, and one has serious physical symptoms to contend with. In addition, hypertension is greatly aggravated by the use of alcohol, for when the brief euphoria at the onset passes, the system swings back in the opposite direction, causing a tendency to greater fear, worry and tension. What is more, the regular use of alcohol is a known cause of chronic depression; it also creates more things to become depressed about as relationships, achievements and self-image deteriorate.

It should be clear, then, that alcohol covers the symptoms of stress only temporarily; in the last analysis it creates more stress. Far more dangerous, however, is the fact that it suppresses the awareness and inner strength needed to solve the situations and personal tendencies which caused the stress in the first place.

Serious as it is, alcohol is only the most obvious of our drug problems. Far more pervasive is that of addiction to prescribed drugs. For instance, how many people do you know who are taking tranquilizers or antidepressants? Probably quite a few, for one of the most serious drug problems we have is the use of medications to mask or suppress the symptoms of stress. Billions of dollars are spent every year on the use of tranquilizers in order to help people relax; for instance, the National Commission on Marijuana and Drug Abuse reports that one of every six Americans takes tranquilizers. The end results are dulled mental faculties and a psychological and physical dependency on the drug. So serious is this problem that the medical profession has recently been forced to reexamine its continued reliance on addictive tranquilizers (which are now classified as Class A narcotics).

Yet we regularly introduce antidepressants and tranquilizers as well as a host of other drugs—sleeping tablets, aspirin, bicarbonate of soda and antacid tablets—into our bodies. Powerful pain-relievers can mask almost any pain, powerful tranquilizers can induce muscle relaxation, and powerful mood elevators can compensate for depression. There are even tablets which allow you to mask the adverse reactions if you overeat, overdrink and completely indulge yourself. Then, when your internal systems complain—"plop, plop, fizz, fizz"—you get symptomatic relief. Yet the chemicals you have just introduced into your body do not actually remove toxic conditions. All that they have done is make you insensitive to them.

Treating the symptom has rarely altered the causal process underlying stress. For example, aspirin and other pain killers do not cure a headache, nor do tranquilizers cure chronic anxiety. They only alleviate the symptoms which are the result of the stress that has been generated by one's personality and behavioral habits. When the medicine wears off, the symptoms return unless the origin (stress) has somehow also been relieved. After all, if taking pills "cures" the disease, then why does one have to keep taking them over and over again?

What is more, masking a symptom is dangerous, for the symptom is really a signal that there is an underlying imbalance in the system. To merely relieve it is to remove a clear warning signal that your body is sending you. In other words, taking a pill to alleviate a symptom of stress is very much like driving your car down the road when the oil light comes on. The light is a symptom of a stressful condition inside your car. But instead of dealing directly with the problem (adding more oil), you take a gun and shoot out the light. Presto! No more symptom! Of course your motor is going to burn out. So, too, is your body.

But we conveniently overlook the consequences of taking powerful chemical agents into our systems. Most medications, for instance, have a long list of possible side effects, and by using them we are adding more problems and more stress to our internal systems. One wonders if people would continue to take medications if they were really aware of what they might do to them. For example, it has recently been reported that a drug used to control high blood pressure may be related to the development of cancer, and everyone knows the tragedy of the "Thalidomide" babies. There are many more such stories. Any public library has a copy of the *Physicians Desk Reference* (PDR) which provides complete information on all drugs. If you are curious, look up the possible side effects of some of our more popular medicines. You will be staggered.

By now it should be clear that stress-induced diseases have rarely been cured by medication. At best, drugs will buy you time in which you can learn to understand and alter the internal, mental processes which have created the problems for you, for in the last analysis, sound mental health is a prerequisite to sound physical health.

Psychological Health

Even though the quality of his entire life is dictated by the state of his mind, man spends incredibly little time enhancing, or even maintaining, sound mental health. In fact only recently, with the advent of the humanistic psychologies, has any real effort been made in modern society towards training the whole mind. Reflecting this deep-felt need, many are turning to religion, self-help books and a wide variety of "pop teachers" in order to find some solution to the mental dissatisfaction so prevalent in our society.

The tremendous amount of money spent on psychiatry and tranquilizers is a good indication of the state of our mental health and maturity. Roughly one of every five people seeks some kind of professional help for emotional problems. Many others may need it, but for some reason they cannot or will not seek it. Furthermore, roughly ten percent of the population will be hospitalized at some point in their lives for serious emotional problems. Very few people can claim tranquility for their very own. In our powerful and rich nation, many are dissatisfied.

Let us consider here the effect chronic stress has on mental health. We live in a pressure-cooker atmosphere. Alvin Toffler's *Future Shock* clearly describes the increasing pace of our society and the subsequent emotional costs for those of us who are unable to cope adequately with the time pressures and the rapid changes they bring about. This concept is further reinforced when we remember that one of the major characteristics of the Type A personality, the coronary-prone person, is that he is usually under the pressure of time.

The effects of stress on performance can be studied in any beginning psychology book. Too much stress inhibits creative thinking and creates personal problems; it even dictates management style. If the boss is under stress, this gets passed down the line until nearly everyone around is hunching his shoulders, raising his blood pressure, making his stomach too acidic—or becoming mentally ill. And to what purpose? Does having a nervous breakdown make you think more clearly? The loss of effectiveness that accompanies stress is not easily measurable—partly because it is subtle but mainly because it goes unrecognized. We are not sensitive enough to note the changes.

Creative problem-solving rarely takes place in a stressed mind. And the higher the stress, the more closed the mind becomes, and the more rigid the thinking process becomes. Recent studies by Dr. Elmer Green at the Menninger Clinic suggest that truly creative thinking takes place when the mind is in a state of inner calm. In other words, the great and creative discoveries in science, in the arts and in the corporate office generally come at times when the mind is at peace with itself.

But even if we could detect the subtle loss of effectiveness when we are under stress, how many of us can really calm our minds and let our inner forces begin to work for us? Instead, we often settle for partial effectiveness. In fact, isn't that the norm?

And unfortunately, the stress that prohibits creative

thought is not restricted to work; it is taken home where the family shares in it. What is more, families themselves, instead of being havens of rest, are often sources of stress, for family structure, too, is affected by the same social changes which create pressure on work environments.

Symptoms of Stress

Everyone has his own unique way of expressing stress. While one person will grind his teeth at night, another will develop insomnia, and yet another will become a toe or finger-tapper. Still others may have headaches, ulcers or high blood pressure. But we often do not recognize these symptoms as manifestations of stress. Most of us recognize it when we are under a great deal of pressure. We also seem to be able to recognize it when others show signs of stress. But we pay very little attention to the physical and behavioral symptoms that reflect our own stress levels. In order to focus awareness on this problem, Table 2 lists some of the symptoms that indicate the presence of stress.

There is no scoring for this; it is only a checklist of symptoms that are frequently associated with stress. How many of them do you manifest? Is there any kind of pattern to your symptoms (i.e., do you check mostly physical symptoms)? The more you have checked, the more you should be concerned about your levels of stress.

Research by Richard Rahe has shown that major changes in one's living or work conditions almost always lead to increased levels of stress. In fact, some researchers have constructed lists of what are called life and organizational changes. These do not necessarily have to be unpleasant, for change in itself provides some degree of instability. For example, if you have changed jobs, moved, gotten married or divorced, had a death in the family, gone on an extended vacation and changed your living habits all within the past twelve months, you are probably going through what Holmes and Rahe call a major life crisis. And the more drastic and numerous the changes, the greater the potential for stress.

The most sensitive indicators of stress are our minds and bodies—but we need to learn to pay attention to them, and few of us have ever learned to objectively study our stream of consciousness. If, however, we could become aware of the reality within—the sensations, bodily feelings and emotional patterns that are there—we could take the necessary steps to alleviate whatever stress we find. Because we have not done this we are paying a tremendous price for the hectic lives we lead.

For example, in 1979 *Time* magazine reported that the cost of health care in 1979 would exceed 206 billion dollars, an increase of sixty-two percent over 1975 expenditures and triple the amount paid only a decade before. Health insurance premiums paid by companies have gone up ten to twenty-five percent (or more) a year. These figures don't even begin to reflect the cost to us in terms of personal effectiveness and personal satisfaction. They are only crude indicators of what these costs are—and stress underlies almost every illness. Table 3 will give you some idea of its specific costs.

Motivation, Arousal and Stress

Even though we know the price we pay for it is high,

TABLE 2
STRESS SYMPTOMS CHECK LIST

_____ 1.Expression of boredom with much or everything
_____ 2.Tendency to begin vacillating in decision making
_____ 3. Tendency to become distraught with trifles
_____ 4. Inattentiveness: loss of power to concentrate
_____ 5. Irritability
_____ 6. Procrastination
_____ 7. Feelings of Persecution
_____ 8. Gut-level feelings of unexplainable dissatisfaction
_____ 9. Forgetfulness
_____10. Tendency to misjudge people
_____11. Uncertain about whom to trust
_____12. Inability to organize self
_____13. Inner confusion about duties or roles
_____14. Loss of appetite
_____15. Loss of energy
_____16. Noticeable loss of weight
_____17. Change of appearance (decline/improvement in dress,
         complexion, etc.)
_____18. Difficulty breathing
_____19. Change of smoking habits
_____20. Change in the use of alcohol
_____21. Allergies or new allergies
_____22. Change in facial expression
_____23. Change in social habits
_____24. Not going to work or home according to past schedule
_____25. Change in life situation (marriage, birth of baby, divorce,
         or death of close relative)
_____26. Waking up in middle of night
_____27. Going back to work at night or on weekends; bringing
         a lot of work home
_____28. Increase in heart rate
_____29. Increase in perspiration; flushed face

____30. Areas of body feel painful, stiff (eyes, neck and shoulders, throat, chest, low back, hands)
____31. Difficulty falling asleep
____32. Poor body posture
____33. Unwilling to laugh at oneself, take oneself too seriously
____34. Increased frequency of infections or colds
____35. High or low blood pressure
____36. "Accident prone"
____37. Nervous habits (tics, smoking, eating, buying, drinking, drugs, compulsive behavior)
____38. Difficulty doing nothing
____39. Bruxism—grinding teeth
____40. Afternoon "poop-out"
____41. Frequent headaches
____42. Decreased enjoyment of sex
____43. Difficulty expressing an emotion
____44. Difficulty being present with others, especially when they are "emoting"
____45. Rigidity in part of body or behavior pattern when specific situation occurs
____46. Experience flooding of thoughts, memories, fantasies when specific emotion or situation arises
____47. Experience "no feelings" in emotional situation
____48. Can't stand to see specific person, place or thing
____49. Recurrent physical disorder
____50. "Over-reacting" to situations
____51. Feel like a pressure cooker about to explode
____52. Paper-shuffling instead of being able to work

TABLE 3
STRESS FACTS: A REFLECTION OF
THE HIGH COST OF STRESS

The following are some facts about our health and related costs. General references are given. All statements are reflections in some way of the effects of stress on our bodies, our actions, and our wallets.

1. Heart and blood vessel diseases will cost the nation an estimated $40.8 billion in 1980.
American Heart Association "Heart Facts"

2. Cardiovascular disease is responsible for nearly one million deaths per year—amounting to 52% of deaths from all causes.
American Heart Association "Heart Facts"

3. Cardiovascular disease is responsible for a loss to national productivity of more than 52 million man-days per year.
American Heart Association "Heart Disease is Your Business"

4. About 34 million Americans have high blood pressure.
American Heart Association "We're Putting Our Heart Into Your Health"

5. Americans consume nearly 15 tons of aspirins per day.
Dr. Roger Williams, Author of *Nutrition Against Disease*

6. One out of every six Americans takes some form of tranquilizer regularly.
U.S. Committee on Drug Abuse

7. The most prescribed drug in the U.S. is Valium, the second most prescribed drug is Librium.
U.S. Committee on Drug Abuse

8. A conservative estimate is that ten percent of the work force can be labeled as either alcoholic or as problem drinkers.
Report to the National Institute on Alcohol Abuse and Alcoholism

9. Alcoholism costs $13 billion for health and medical costs, and $20 billion for lost production costs.
Report to the National Institute on Alcohol Abuse and Alcoholism

10. Americans spend a greater share of their resources on health care than do the people of any other nation.
U.S. News and World Report

11. Americans spend $1 out of every $9 on health care.
U.S. Department of Health, Education and Welfare

12. Hospitals have an increased cost average of seventeen percent per year.
U.S. Department of Labor

we often assume that we need to be under stress in order to achieve high levels of performance. It is also a common belief that competition is necessary in order to motivate increased efficiency. But at what levels of competition does the accompanying stress become an interference? Very few of us are able to moderate our drive to compete in order not to suffer from it. Very few of us can alleviate the pressure built up from competition without further stressing our bodies with hard, physical exercises. We have learned to be either very active or very passive, but not tranquil or balanced.

Years of psychological research show that stress does interfere with performance. Years of psychological research also show that stress is a necessary stimulus to high performance. What are we to believe? The problem lies in the fact that we confuse the terms *motivation, arousal* and *stress*. Motivation is the key to high achievement, and of course arousal is also necessary or we would accomplish very little. There are, however, vast differences between high states of directed motivation and arousal, and the unregulated arousal which results in stress. To attempt to eliminate arousal would certainly prove harmful. But we can learn to eliminate that process by which arousal turns into stress.

This is not to say that we will be able to eliminate time pressures, or that we should (or even can) eliminate competition, or that hard physical exercise is harmful. The point is that we must learn to control our responses to them. We cannot easily change our work structures or our social structures, but we can easily change our internal response to the pressures generated by these structures. That is the key to successful stress management.

For example, the work of Dr. Abraham Maslow with

those who have achieved high degrees of psychological maturity (a process called self-actualization) has shown that such people do not create the same degree of stress for themselves as others do. In addition, they suffer from fewer illnesses and they show consistently higher levels of satisfaction with life. Yet many of them hold high positions in stress-related jobs. Self-actualized people, in fact, usually find joy in their work, openly express their feelings to their family and friends and are not afraid to compliment and help others. In fact, they take joy in another's achievements. They are not threatened by another's success, even if he is a competitor. They are secure in themselves and confident of their own ability to handle whatever life may deal them. They are not desperate to have "fun," to "make it" professionally, to go further than the Joneses, or to control others. Yet these self-actualized people are consistently high achievers. What is more, they do it in the same "pressure cooker" that exists for everyone else in our society. In short, they are living examples that stress and its associated tension, worry, anxiety and "nerves" are not necessary ingredients for high achievement and performance. They have learned how to manage stress.

Holistic Medicine and Biofeedback

It is unfortunate that most treatment for psychosomatic disease is directed overwhelmingly towards giving symptomatic relief. It is equally unfortunate that treatment is palliative, directed toward suppressing or eliminating the symptoms of disease, and that very little is being done to cure and remove the root causes. And this is the traditional medical approach.

There is a fascinating therapeutic approach, however, currently developing in this country, which takes into account all aspects of the individual—physical, mental and spiritual. Holistic medicine, as this is called, involves a comprehensive framework for understanding human behavior in which all areas of health—diet, exercise, habits and beliefs, to name a few, are integrated into a meaningful pattern. Holistic medicine is not, however, nor should it be, a hodgepodge of techniques without a unifying philosophy or framework behind it. Moreover, it is a truly interdisciplinary approach to health which places the responsibility and the tools for increased well-being with the individual. Holistic health is ultimately a self-training program, for it is this alone that can root out the causes of stress.

One important tool of holistic medicine is biofeedback, the use of sophisticated electronic instruments by which an ongoing physiological process (such as muscle tension or pulse rate) can be monitored and converted into a recognizable signal which is then given back to the subject who is being monitored. The instrument acts like a mirror, giving one immediate information about what is happening inside his body. Its therapeutic effect stems from the fact that it provides the opportunity for one to become aware of and control those physiological and mental patterns which result in a psychosomatic dysfunction. In other words, it helps one to develop increased self-awareness and self-control.

An example of how a biofeedback therapy program works is reported in *Meditational Therapy* (see bibliography). In this program, the patients learned to eliminate chronic tension headaches within a six-week period. The patients studied had suffered from severe headaches for twenty to thirty years without finding any consistent relief. This means that for twenty or thirty years they had been taking a wide variety of medications that were only partly successful in masking the pain and not at all successful in curing the disease. After an average of only six weeks of stress reduction training through relaxation, breathing exercises, meditation and biofeedback training, the symptoms were entirely gone. No drugs were necessary. In fact, the patients stopped taking the drugs they had been using previously. These were no longer necessary because the symptoms were no longer there. In other words, *when the pattern of stress was altered, the symptoms were removed.* The symptoms were not the problem; the underlying stress was.

Biofeedback therapy is equally successful in treating many other diseases that are related to stress. For example, Dr. Chandra Patel in England has shown that a combination of biofeedback, relaxation and yoga breathing exercises have been used to successfully reduce high blood pressure, a potentially much more serious problem than headache. This therapy is successful because it works not only with the symptoms but also with the primary cause—stress.

Another advantage to biofeedback training is the reduction of medication needed in order to control the symptoms of disease. This is an invaluable benefit, for as we have seen, the drugs used to provide symptomatic relief can often cause side effects which are sometimes more serious than the target symptoms themselves. There is only one possible side effect to biofeedback; during repeated training sessions the trainee can come in touch with certain deep internal states which may be emotionally troublesome.

However, given the nature of the training, he is able to handle any situation himself, without external help.

A holistic approach to our health problems, then, offers us real hope that we can reduce stress to negligible levels through our own efforts. And this, in turn can free us to unlock our inner creative potential which is badly needed to solve the tremendous social and economic problems we face. If we were stress-free we could indeed transform our society.

The experts can tell you about stress, but you experience it every day. You alone can determine its effect on your body, your mind, your work, your interrelationships—indeed, on every level of your life. And you alone can do something about it by learning how to maintain the momentum of modern life yet not be affected by it. For this, the right attitude in daily life is needed—and for the right attitude, inner strength. Unless we can create a bridge between our internal states and our external life, our efforts will be futile.

The solutions to stress problems are amazingly simple. This is not to say that they are easy. But they are available. We need only to experiment personally and see which ones work for us. The first step is to gain knowledge; we must first understand what stress is, how we create it and how we sustain it in our minds and bodies. Then we will understand how to avoid the problem. In the next chapter we will begin by analyzing, on a practical level, just what this monster named stress really is. Don't be surprised to find, as the cartoon strip character Pogo once said, "We have found the enemy—and it is us!"

The Anatomy of Stress-A New Look

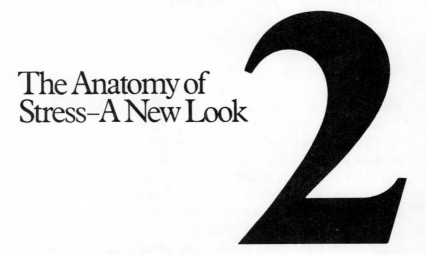

The current confusion about what stress is and how we can be free of it has come about because the terms are not clearly defined, and this stems from the fact that there is no coherent, holistic theory and philosophy of human functioning which can unite the disparate and multifaceted aspects of arousal and stress into a meaningful whole. In other words, our perspective on the subject is too narrow. Our goal here is to resolve this confusion by providing a new and more comprehensive framework by which one can understand and control his own stress response. But if we are looking ultimately to developing individual skill in controlling this, it is vitally important that we have at least a basic understanding of the internal physiological processes which are involved in it. In particular, we need to understand the neurological organization and functions which regulate and control the physiological responses as well as the events and forces which, in turn, influence and control the neurological system. For if we can control the control systems, we can eventually eliminate stress. The first step in this process is to learn something about the fight-or-flight response.

Fight-or-Flight—A Concept Too Narrow

The framework for current studies on stress has evolved primarily from the work of Walter Bradford Cannon and Hans Selye. Beginning in the 1930's, Dr. Selye, expanding on the work of Dr. Cannon, began to explore what happens to living organisms under sustained physiological arousal. His well-known research has shown that when an organism is faced with what it perceives as a threat in the environment an automatic arousal mechanism, called the fight-or-flight response, is activated which puts the body on alert. This response is a mobilization of the body's ability to protect itself, either by action towards the threat (fight) or by action to avoid the threat (flight).

We can relate to this arousal response more clearly if we simply examine our own experiences. Remember the last time that you were driving down a highway and came very close to having a serious accident. There are a variety of feelings, changes and sensations that you may have experienced, including the following:

Increased heart rate
Dramatic changes in your breathing rate
Perspiration or sweaty palms
Nausea, drastic changes in your gastro-intestinal tract
Trembling, or shivers
Emotional changes such as fear or anger

Perceptual changes (perhaps even perceiving in slow
    motion)
Muscle tension
Increased concentration or attention

In fact, many changes were going on in your body at
the time, all relating to a heightened state of physiological
arousal over which you had very little conscious control. It
is important to recognize that this involuntary arousal is
always keyed to the perception of some kind of danger and
involves a wide variety of physiological, biochemical and
neurochemical changes that are mediated primarily by the
activation of the sympathetic nervous system. Table 1
lists the actual physiological events that take place when this
alerting mechanism is activated. Increased muscle tone, heart
rate and blood pressure as well as increased respiratory rate
and increased endocrine function are just a few of the many
changes that take place during the fight-or-flight response.
Consistent changes in the vascular system and hormonal
balance also accompany this pattern. In fact, so many internal changes take place when this response is strongly
activated that it is often referred to as an autonomic storm.

In the initial phase, however, the fight-or-flight
response appears to be beneficial, as it alerts the organism
and provides it with extra strength on many levels. Not only
does the body get ready for action, but the mental faculties
are also sharpened, increasing concentration, perceptual
acuity and mental clarity. Obviously this is necessary if
action is to be taken.

As Dr. Selye continued his research, however, it
became increasingly apparent that the fight-or-flight response

TABLE 1
INTERNAL CHANGES OCCURRING DURING
THE FIGHT/FLIGHT AROUSAL RESPONSE

Increased sugar and fats enter the bloodstream to provide more fuel for quick energy.

Increased breathing rate increases oxygen supply in the blood.

Increased heart rate and blood pressure insure sufficient blood supply to the cells.

Blood-clotting mechanisms are activated to protect against injury.

Increased muscle tone (tension) prepares the body for action.

Increased pituitary functioning stimulates endocrine production of the hormones; adrenalin and glucagon production increases.

Digestive processes shut down; blood is diverted to muscles and the brain (Peristalsis decreases and digestive enzymes are decreased.)

Pupils are dilated, allowing more light to enter the eye.

Attention and alertness increase.

was merely a part of a more involved process, for the alarm response did not automatically limit itself and return to a non-aroused state. In addition, the research clearly demonstrated that when arousal is maintained over an extended period of time, the physiological systems begin to break down and undergo pathological changes. This signifies a disease state which eventually ends in death to the organism. This entire process, which Dr. Selye calls the General Adaptation Syndrome, can be placed into four fairly distinct phases:

Alarm: This is the fight-or-flight response triggered by a perceived threat to the organism (the autonomic storm of physiological arousal).

Resistence: This is the stage in which the body attempts to adapt to (and compensate for) the physiological changes occurring from the alarm stage. It is an attempt to regain homeostasis.

Exhaustion: If the arousal continues, the body's attempt to create a balance as well as the effects of the alarm arousal lead to a depletion of reserve fuel and to a state of exhaustion. Physiological systems begin to break down.

Termination: If there is no relief from the arousal, the resultant stress on the physiological systems leads to the death of the organism.

In other words, when an organism remains, for whatever reason, in a state of constant arousal (or what is often referred to as stress), the organism literally wears itself out.

Continued work by Dr. Selye and others led to the recognition that the same physiological arousal pattern characterizes both the alarm reaction (the fight-or-flight response) and high positive states of arousal. For instance, engaging in any challenging event results in physiological arousal, and it is obvious that these states are not necessarily negative. Without arousal, for instance, we could never achieve, there would be no knowledge gained, and no challenges met. However, the relationship between arousal and stress has not been properly understood and has led to the confusion involving "good stress" and "bad stress."

Equating arousal and stress has led to a confusion of concepts, terms and theories. Dr. Selye now refers to any nonspecific arousal in the body as stress, calling the maladaptive use of arousal "distress" and the adaptive use of arousal "eustress." The difficulty with this concept, however, lies in determining just what makes arousal useful (or adaptive) in one instance and leads to disease in the next. Is there really "good" stress? Is stress really necessary?

Dr. Selye's pioneering work in the field of stress is invaluable. His theory, however, contains two fundamental errors that make it increasingly inadequate. In the first place, it is based on research which deals primarily with arousal mediated directly through the sympathetic division of the autonomic nervous system. The resultant research has led most authors and researchers to incorrectly assume that stress has to do with states of sympathetic arousal only; the parasympathetic system is not adequately taken into account except in the sense that stress-related problems are thought to be solved through the activation of that system (the "relaxation response"). This one-sided approach to auto-nomic functioning is unnecessarily limiting, for it has pre-vented us from understanding the true nature of stress.

The second difficulty with Dr. Selye's theory is that it is inherently tied to the incorrect idea that autonomic func-tioning is autonomous—that it is not amenable to conscious control and direction. Consequently, it has by and large ignored the powerful and ultimately determinent role played by higher cortical activity in stress management. More impor-tant, it does not account for the role of will and awareness in the control and regulation of this autonomic system. Thus, according to Dr. Selye, stress is an unavoidable consequence of our life.

On the contrary, however, we can be free of stress once we understand that it includes both functions of the autonomic system equally and does indeed allow for the intervention of our higher cortical activities in controlling it. As we shall see in later chapters, we do not have to be help-less slaves to our nervous system.

There is an alternative way of approaching the problem which eliminates the confusion between "good" stress and "bad" stress. What is more, it leads to direct and conscious control over the arousal response. But first we must look at our physiological functions from a perspective which in-volves all of the nervous system. We must understand how changes in the body are brought about and realize that the mind and body are interconnected and function very closely together.

For example, whenever there is an image or thought in the mind, the body is immediately programmed to perform the actions implicit in that thought or image. The degree (or intensity) of the programming and resultant physiological change is determined by the level of emotional involvement. For example, if we think of a particular food, the body will begin to prepare itself for eating and digestion. Saliva will flow, making the mouth "water," intestinal activity will increase and the stomach may rumble. The degree to which these preparatory physical changes take place depends on how long or how frequently the thought of food is entertained and how intense the thought is (how strong the appetite or craving is, or how much we are emotionally involved with the thought). If it is a fleeting thought and the mind goes on to other images, then the bodily preparation for digestion will be fleeting and it will begin to make appropriate responses to subsequent images or thoughts.

This interaction between body and mind is reciprocal. As the body responds to the image of food, for instance, sensations of hunger and appetite will reinforce the mind's tendency to think about food, and this, in turn, will strengthen or intensify physical changes. Thus, a feedback-feedforward cycle of mutual reinforcement (or cause and effect) is established between the mind and body until an action is taken (such as eating) which fulfills the sensation of hunger and quiets the appetite.

As we shall see later, the activation of the body's mechanisms need not depend on an actual event in the environment. One does not have to see, smell, taste or touch food or even hear sounds connected with food in order to alter his physiological state. All he needs to do is think about food or have images of it in his mind. By the same token, just thinking about exercise (such as running on a treadmill) can create increased heart rate and blood pressure, increased respiratory rate and increased flow of blood to the muscles. While this subject is not directly considered until the next chapter, keep in mind that it is the mind acting through the brain which ultimately controls all of the physiological responses—including neurological and glandular responses.

Our Nerves

Our nervous system is the primary regulator of the body's responses. It is made up of nerve cells specialized to transmit electrical impulses much as electric wires do. On one end are specialized surfaces (called dendrites) for receiving impulses from other nerves, while the other end is a long filament (called an axon) which carries the impulse to another nerve in the chain. Figure 1 illustrates this relationship. Nerves also carry electrical impulses (of less than 1/10 of a volt) to glands to modify their level of secretion, as well as to muscles to control their contraction and relaxation.

There are three basic types of nerves. Motor nerves (Figure 2) lead to muscles or glands and control their actions, and sensory nerves (Figure 3) respond to changes either in the external environment or within the body. For example, our sense of touch, pain or temperature comes from specialized sensory organs in the skin which generate impulses which are then conducted along sensory nerves. All of our sense organs convert sensations into complex patterns of electrical impulses which are then transmitted by these nerves. There are also internuncial (or association) nerves (Figure 4) which transmit impulses from one nerve to another.

Nerves make contact with each other at a transfer

Figure 1
AUTONOMIC MOTOR NEURON

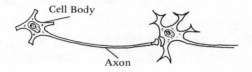

Cell Body

Axon

Figure 2
SOMATIC MOTOR NEURON

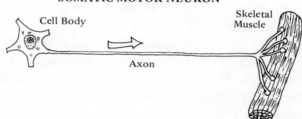

Cell Body

Skeletal
Muscle

Axon

Figure 3
SENSORY NEURON

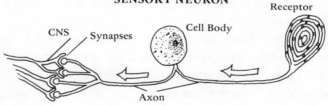

Receptor

CNS   Synapses

Cell Body

Axon

Figure 4
ASSOCIATION NEURON (INTERNEURON)

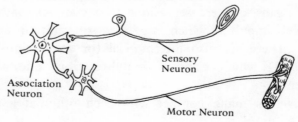

Sensory
Neuron

Association
Neuron

Motor Neuron

point called a synapse. This is where the electrical current is passed from the axon of the nerve carrying the impulse to the dendrite of the second nerve—which then receives the impulse. This transfer, however, is not electrical, but chemical; what happens is that as the electrical impulse arrives at the end of the axon, it causes the release of small packets of a chemical called acetylcholine (ACH) which is stored in the nerve endings. As shown in Figure 5, these molecules are then discharged into the fluid surrounding the axon and drift away in all directions. In the nearby dendrite the ACH molecules attach themselves to special receptors, and when enough have been collected the nerve membrane in the dendrite changes to release the stored electric charge (or impulse). This is now transmitted along the second nerve to the next nerve and synapse. The ACH then drifts away from the dendrite back into the surrounding fluid where it is broken down by a special protein enzyme called cholinesterase.

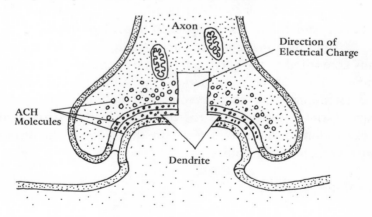

Figure 5
THE SYNAPSE

This same process occurs at the junction between a nerve and a muscle. Here, the nerve impulse causes the release of ACH from the end of the axon; this ACH then migrates to the muscle membrane where it attaches to receptors and causes the membrane to become "leaky," thus unleashing a stored electrical charge. This, in turn, causes the release of stored calcium into the inner fluid of the muscle cells surrounding the muscle fibrils. The calcium then helps to form a bridge between the fibrils, pulling them closer together and causing the muscle as a whole to contract.

Acetylcholine (only one of many molecules called neurotransmitters) is the transmitter where a nerve joins a skeletal muscle; it is also the transmitter in many nerve synapses of the brain and spinal cord. Other molecules can serve a similar role. Norepinephrine, for instance, a close relative of epinephrine and adrenalin, is the transmitter in the sympathetic nervous system and probably in parts of the brain. Other molecules such as serotonin and dopamine also act as transmitters in certain specialized parts of the brain.

The functional components of the nervous system are thus comprised of the nerve cell (with its axon and dendrites) and the junction between nerves (the synapse). The key to understanding how the nervous system works, however, particularly in relationship to stress, lies in the patterns of organization of the nerves and how they control the different functions of our bodies.

The Reflex Arc

The most basic neural organization is the reflex arc, found in its simplest form in the muscle stretch reflex. This unit is composed of one sensory nerve leading from a muscle or tendon into the spinal cord, one motor nerve leading from the spinal cord to the same muscle, and often an internuncial nerve which is entirely within the spinal cord and which connects the sensory and motor nerves. The sensory nerve monitors the degree of stretch in the muscle, and if it is stretched too far, or too quickly, the sensory nerve will be activated and generate an impulse. This is transmitted along the sensory nerve, through the internuncial nerve, into the motor nerve. The impulse is then returned by the motor nerve back to the muscle, causing the muscle to contract. This reflex contraction automatically protects the muscle against being overstretched and possibly damaged.

The knee-jerk reflex, which a doctor tests by striking one's knee below the kneecap, is an example of this reflex arc. Here, the tendon from the powerful quadriceps muscle (forming the front of the thigh) extends over the front of the knee and is inserted into the tibia bone of the lower leg. Striking this tendon causes the muscle to stretch very suddenly and thus elicit a reflex contraction of the quadricep thigh muscle which results in a brief kicking motion or knee jerk. Figure 6 illustrates this basic reflex arc pathway.

There are many such protective reflex actions, some of which are quite complex. For example, the startle response involves a much wider response. Here a sensory nerve connected with the ear, for instance, receives information from sound receptors in the ear; the resulting impulse is transmitted through an intermediate nerve system which connects to many different motor nerves. This causes them to fire together in an organized pattern, and this in turn causes us to startle, taking in a small rapid breath and contracting

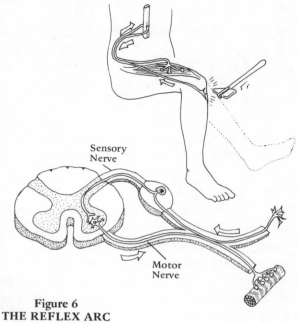

Figure 6
THE REFLEX ARC

certain muscles in order to move away from the source of the stimulus.

While the stretch, or knee-jerk, reflex occurs along a very simple pathway, it does not function in isolation. Several factors influence its sensitivity, including how much stretch or how rapid a stretch will cause the reflex to occur. Those whose "nerves are on edge," who are jumpy or irritable, or who are hyperactive, tend to respond to even the slightest physical or emotional stimulus with a rapid and accentuated muscular, or verbal, or emotional response. This "nervousness" often shows itself in strong reflexes. For instance, in these people a small strike of the reflex hammer on the quadriceps tendon will elicit a very brisk, accentuated kick-ing motion, and startle responses of such people tend to be quite exaggerated. There are others, however, who seem almost depressed, not reacting to many stimuli at all. Simi-larly, their reflex responses often appear to be suppressed, and even strong taps on the tendons fail to elicit a reflex response.

What is important is that this reflexive stretch response can be modified and influenced by several different factors. The stretch receptor (or sensory nerve) in a muscle is called a muscle spindle and rests among the muscle fibers. It is very much like a miniature muscle in that it can also contract and relax. It is embedded in the muscle so that if that muscle is stretched, the spindle is also stretched. However, it is impor-tant to note that the spindle's state of tension or relaxation can be modified or altered independently from the motion of the muscle, by signals emerging from the brain and spinal cord.

A muscle spindle that is in a relaxed state requires much more stretching on the part of the parent muscle to generate enough impulses to initiate the reflex arc. Con-versely, a spindle under tension, (or in a more contracted state) will initiate reflex arcs with only small stretches of the muscle. So learning to decrease the activity of muscle spindle systems is an effective way to reduce overall muscle tension in the body. In actuality, muscle spindles are constantly emitting impulses, but they fire more rapidly when they are being stretched. The lower level of impulses created when the spindle is at rest is partly responsible for what is called the tone of the muscle (its degree of relaxation or tension).

The muscle, when contracted (or put into a state of

tension) does not act in isolation, for there are many internal events that also occur to facilitate and support this action. Thus, when muscles are contracted through reflexive responses or in readiness to carry out actions required by mental images, the rest of the body must also prepare itself to support that muscular activity. At such times fuel from food in the form of glucose and fatty acids, along with oxygen to burn the fuel, must go to the muscles preferentially. This requires decreasing the activity of certain less immediately-needed body processes—such as digestion in the intestines, liver and pancreas function, or excretion from the kidneys. As a result, both the activity of these organs and the blood flow to them decreases. At the same time changes take place in the heart and respiratory system. The heart beats faster and with more force, and if it is not accompanied by vigorous muscle exertion, this could lead to an elevation of blood pressure. At the same time the respiratory rate increases; its pattern begins to show predominantly chest breathing in order to draw on the reserve capacity of the lungs. This allows for a greater transport of oxygen into the circulation as well as a greater elimination of carbon dioxide.

These patterns will take place most intensely when the body undertakes strenuous muscular exertion, and they occur in a very carefully modulated sequence in proportion to the degree of exertion. In addition, they occur, although to a lesser degree, in the absence of specific muscular activity but as preparation for it. It is important to understand that these changes also seem to take place on a moment-to-moment basis as a preparatory reflex to mental thoughts and imagery that may require muscular activity. As we shall see, the degree of change is related to the frequency, intensity and duration of the specific mental image. This is a crucial factor in understanding stress.

The Functional Structures of the Nervous System

It is our nervous system (along with parts of the endocrine, or glandular, system) which holds the major responsibility for organizing bodily changes. As shown in Figure 7, the nervous system is composed of two major divisions, the central nervous system (CNS), which involves the brain and the spinal cord, and the peripheral nervous system (PNS), comprising all of the nerve tissue in the rest of the body that leads to and from the central nervous system. Ultimate control of the nervous system rests in the CNS, particularly in the brain; the role of the peripheral nervous system is to relay messages to and from the brain and different parts of the body so that it can act in a coordinated, efficient manner and carry out our mental goals.

The peripheral nervous system has two major divisions. The sensory-motor component, called the voluntary nervous system, is responsible for carrying sensory data or impulses from our sensory organs (via sensory nerves) which thus receive information about the outside world as well as about the state of the muscles and joints; it also transmits impulses back to the musculo-skeletal system (via motor nerves) which control muscular contraction and body motion. It has major connections in the most advanced part of our brain, the cerebral cortex, which is associated with conscious (or voluntary) behavior, free will, or choice.

The second major division of the peripheral nervous system is called the autonomic nervous system because it has

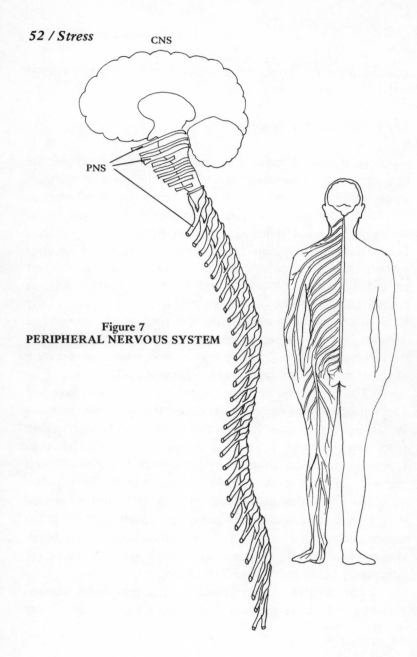

Figure 7
PERIPHERAL NERVOUS SYSTEM

the capacity to function autonomously (or on its own without conscious control) and below the threshold of our usual conscious awareness. Its function is to organize and regulate the functioning of the glands, skin, heart, lungs, digestive organs and excretory organs as well as to coordinate their activity in whatever directions and tasks the mind and brain have established. This includes tasks such as eating, resting, digestion and exercise. Like the muscular system, regulated by the sensory-motor division, it is extremely responsive to mental imagery or thoughts. Not many years ago it was thought that the autonomic nervous system could not be controlled through conscious effort, but it is important to understand that this is not so. A great deal of conscious control can be exercised over it by controlling certain types of stimuli or by certain mental images. This is useful and necessary for effective control of stress.

The autonomic nervous system is, in turn, divided into two functional systems. One mediates the inner, physiological aspects of arousal and is associated with outward activity involving muscular exertion and large expenditures of energy. It is called the sympathetic system because it controls inner body functions to go along with, or in sympathy with, outward oriented activity.

The other division of the autonomic nervous system, associated in part with relaxation, regulates the housekeeping work of the body and is called the parasympathetic system. Its focus is on the inward activities of nourishment and excretion, repairing tissues and building up energy and fuel supplies for the next period of outward action. Table 2 gives a brief overview of the effects of activating the sympathetic and parasympathetic systems.

TABLE 2
THE EFFECTS OF AUTONOMIC ACTIVITY

	Physiological Effects	Behavioral Effects
Sympathetic Dominance	Increased cardiac rate, blood pressure, sweat secretion; pupillary dilation; inhibition of gastro-intestinal motor and secretory function.	Arousal, alertness, heightened activity and emotional responsiveness.
	Desynchrony of EEG, increased skeletal muscle tone, elevation of certain hormones—adrenaline, noradrenaline, adrenocortical steroids, thyroxin.	
Parasympathetic Dominance	Reduction in cardiac rate, blood pressure, sweat secretion; pupillary constriction; increased gastro-intestinal motor and secretory function.	Inactivity, digestion, relaxation, drowsiness and sleep.
	Synchrony of EEG, loss of skeletal muscle tone, blocking of shivering response, increased secretion of insulin.	

Anatomically, the two systems are distinct. The nerve fibers of the sympathetic system originate from nerve centers in the brain, course down within lateral parts of the spinal cord, and leave the spinal canal through gaps between adjacent vertebrae in the chest and upper lumbar areas. As shown in Figure 8, these nerves, once outside the spinal column, travel up and down the outside of the vertebrae and interconnect in dense concentrations of nerve tissue called ganglia.

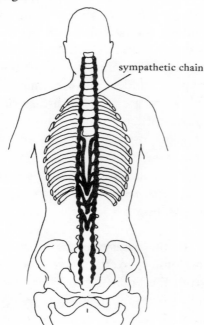

sympathetic chain

Figure 8
THE SYMPATHETIC
NERVOUS SYSTEM

The nerves and their areas of interconnection extend along the vertebrae on both sides from the neck to the pelvic area. Separate nerve fibers then leave the ganglia and course into the body where they stimulate the various organs to prepare for action—increasing heart rate, increasing the diameter of the lung airways, increasing the size of the pupil to allow more light to enter the eye, increasing activity of certain sweat glands to allow for efficient dissipation of heat generated by muscular work, decreasing function of the digestive and excretory organs, constricting blood vessles in areas where blood is not needed and opening vessels in areas where it is needed. Figure 9 illustrates the nerve connections to the various organs.

The sympathetic system is activated in case of sudden life-threatening emergencies, so it has the capacity to function on a moment's notice, emitting a sudden, large and coordinated discharge. It is the extensive interconnections of all the nerve fibers in the ganglia along the spinal column that give it this ability. But this sensitivity, while very useful, has a definite drawback. Though its evolution has made it possible for us to protect ourselves against sudden physical threats requiring large muscular movements, the threats we experience daily do not require sudden massive muscular activity for their resolution. They are mostly threats of a mental and emotional nature, often requiring no major muscular action at all. Yet the sensitive triggering of the sympathetic system takes place in response to the intense threat that was perceived, and we are left in a bodily state that is inappropriate to the circumstances--a state from which there is often no effective means for release. This is a major component of stress.

As shown in Figure 10, the parasympathetic system has an entirely different anatomic pattern. Nerve fibers in this system travel to and from the brain in the spinal cord, leaving the vertebral column above and below the sympathetic channels, through the neck vertebrae and through the lower lumbar and sacral vertebrae. The major parasympathetic nerve, the vagus nerve, branches off inside the skull and is called the tenth cranial nerve. It contains almost eighty percent of the nerve fibers of the parasympathetic system.

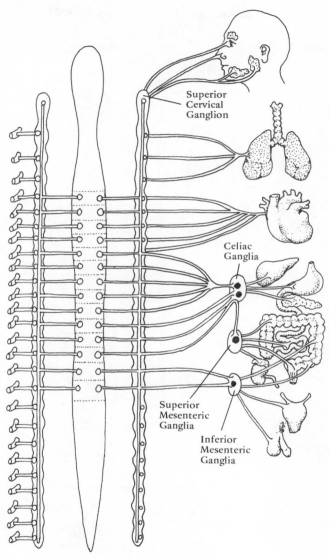

Superior
Cervical
Ganglion

Celiac
Ganglia

Superior
Mesenteric
Ganglia

Inferior
Mesenteric
Ganglia

Figure 9
SCHEME OF SYMPATHETIC NERVOUS SYSTEM

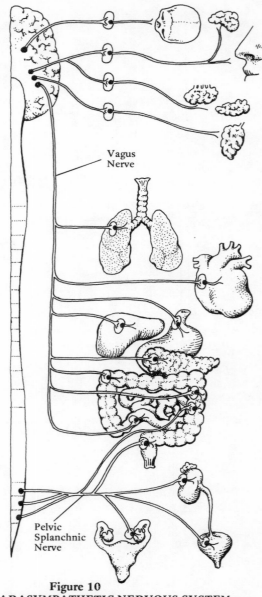

Vagus
Nerve

Pelvic
Splanchnic
Nerve

Figure 10
SCHEME OF PARASYMPATHETIC NERVOUS SYSTEM

The right and left vagus nerves, named from a Latin root meaning "to wander," leave the brain from within the skull. On their journey down into the abdomen they send branches to the throat area, the lungs, the heart and the upper stomach. The left vagus nerve stops at the upper stomach, but the right vagus nerve sends out fibers which continue into the abdominal cavity to the small intestines, parts of the large colon and other organs concerned with digestion. The right vagus nerve actually terminates in the coeliac ganglion. Nerve transmissions, however, from this nerve continue throughout the rest of the digestive tract by virtue of the synapses there.

An extensive area of parasympathetic control is thus associated with the two vagus nerves, and in particular, with the right vagus nerve. Unlike the sympathetic nerves, these nerves do not immediately rejoin and interconnect in ganglia along the spinal column; they course into the body, forming interconnections in ganglia very close to the organ they innervate. For example, the parasympathetic nerves that reach into the large intestine have their ganglia within the muscular wall of the intestine itself, allowing for a localized coordination of activity. This is in keeping with the several functions the parasympathetic system must undertake in its housekeeping role. Parasympathetic stimulation, then, may coordinate bladder or rectal function independently, without a marked change in parasympathetic influence on the heart or salivary glands.

While the sympathetic and parasympathetic systems have different anatomical structures, with remarkably different capabilities, they have many areas in common. In fact, the nerves of the two systems are intricately intertwined and work in harmony. This close relationship is reflected physically in localized groupings, called nerve plexuses. These are made up of nerves from the sympathetic system (post-ganglionic fibers) that have come from the points of interconnection in their ganglia together with nerves from the parasympathetic system (pre-ganglionic fibers) that are on their way from the spinal cord to their various ganglia closer to the individual organs.

These nerve plexuses are found along the vertical axis of the body from the base of the spine to the head, in front of the vertebral column. They include the sacral plexus (comprised of nerves controlling bowel, bladder and sexual function), the lumbar plexus (made up of nerves associated with large bowel and kidney function), the solar plexus (associated with control of the digestive organs of the spleen, pancreas, stomach and small bowel), the cardiac plexus (involving heart function), and the laryngeal plexus (innervating the larynx, thyroid and parathyroid glands).

It is interesting to note that no specific function has been associated with these plexuses, since the nerves running through them do not connect (or synapse) with each other as they do in ganglia. However, nerves do have some characteristics in common with wires carrying intermittent currents. They generate small electromagnetic fields, and when a high concentration of nerves exists as well as some synchrony in their firing patterns (as happens in the cerebral cortex), then the field is large enough to be measured. It is known that the electromagnetic field around one wire can influence the current-carrying ability of another nearby wire. Thus, a strong possibility exists that even when there are no specific anatomic interconnections between the nerves in a plexus, a degree of mutual influence and interaction may take place through the electromagnetic fields they create. (It may be possible to detect this with extremely sensitive instrumentation.) The strength of the fields of individual plexuses may also depend on the degree of coordination (or synchrony) among the firings of the individual nerves.

The sympathetic and parasympathetic nervous systems function in a very close, cooperative relationship, working together in such a way as to contribute to the overall equilibrium (or homeostasis) of the organs they supply—and in general, the organs are supplied with nerves from both systems. This is called reciprocal innervation. For example, both systems innervate the heart. The effect of parasympathetic stimulation (through the vagus nerve) is to slow the heartbeat; the effect of sympathetic stimulation is to speed it up. At rest, both systems discharge at a low level, while the resting heartbeat represents a balance of the two opposing influences. When there is muscular exertion of anxiety, the heart speeds up. This is first accomplished by a decrease in vagal (parasympathetic) activity and then by an increase in sympathetic activity.

In other words, while sympathetic stimulation is keyed to arousal, parasympathetic stimulation is keyed to inhibition, tuning down physiological activity and putting everything on a sort of rest-phase. In healthy functioning these two systems balance each other, exchanging dominance as the need requires but maintaining an equilibrium as dominance shifts. *Understanding this natural balance of autonomic functioning is the key to a comprehensive and functional understanding of stress.*

Arousal, Stress and the Peripheral Nervous Systems

Stress is usually associated with the physiological arousal which is mediated in the autonomic nervous system by sympathetic dominance. That is, in a state of arousal the body is responding to some perceived threat or to some type of inner stimulation which has resulted in the activation of sympathetic discharge and the suppression of parasympathetic discharge. Since our first response to threat is neurological, generally leading to changes that prepare the body to take muscular action, the speed at which the sympathetic system can react is very rapid.

The endocrine, or glandular system, however, must become involved for sustained arousal, for while neurological impulses initiate the autonomic response, continued, or intense, sympathetic discharge is supplemented by hormones released from certain endocrine glands. The adrenal glands are the first. Sitting on top of the kidneys, they are divided into two parts. The inner, called the medulla, stores the hormones epinephrine and norepinephrine, and it is highly innervated with sympathetic nerve fibers. Any increase in sympathetic activation stimulates the medulla to release its two hormones into the bloodstream. (In general, about three times as much epinephrine as norepinephrine is released, although some researchers feel that a greater proportion of norepenephrine is released during fear or anxiety responses, a greater proportion of epinephrine during anger.)

This hormonal release serves several functions. Because the hormone is secreted into, and circulated by, the bloodstream in order to reach its destination, it takes a few seconds longer for an organ to react to hormone stimulation than to direct nerve activation. However, the effect of hormone stimulation will last up to ten times as long, because once the hormone is in the bloodstream it will take longer for the stimulus to disappear. In other words, you can stop firing a nerve instantly, but you can't clear the bloodstream of hormones quite as quickly.

A second effect of hormone release is that every cell in the body can be reached as they circulate in the bloodstream, and this increases the overall rate of cell metabolism, preparing the cells for increased activity. A third effect of hormone release, one that results predominently from epinephrine, is a shift in the body's energy balance through the extra release of glucose and fatty acids into the bloodstream. (This provides the fuel necessary for increased muscular activity.)

The activation of the body's hormonal system occurs in proportion to the duration and intensity of the perceived threat. Very short-lived (or low intensity) stimuli may create no perceptible sympathetic response. A very brief but intense stimulus, such as a sudden fright, however, may cause a reaction in the sympathetic nerves followed by a perceptible surge of epinephrine which may take several minutes or longer to subside. But if the adverse environmental condition is more prolonged and requires adaptive activity to be sustained over hours, or days, or longer, then another sequence of hormonal changes tends to occur in order to sustain and supplement sympathetic nerve function over a prolonged period of high activity.

This adaptation also involves the adrenal gland, for it is the inner adrenal gland (the medulla) that is activated within seconds to minutes and adds additional epinephrine and norepinephrine to the body tissues. Then, after even more prolonged stimulation, lasting over a few hours, the outer part of the adrenal gland (the adrenal cortex) also becomes stimulated. This releases cortisone and related hormones into the blood that supplement and augment the effects of the sympathetic nerves and the circulating epinephrine. It is hours, and even days, however, before its effects take place.

In other words, the effect of nerve responses through the local release of norepinephrine is almost immediate, and the effect of circulating epinephrine on cell membrane takes place in minutes and may last for hours, shifting the gears of all the cells and causing them to become more active. In storage cells, for instance, such as the liver and fat cells, it causes fuel to be released rather than stored. These events use the cell's existing machinery and activate it, utilizing its current capacity. The effect of cortisone, on the other hand, is to build, within the cell, additional new machinery in the form of cellular proteins called enzymes. This extends the limits of the cell, increasing its overall capacity for a particular activity.

Thyroid gland secretion can also increase under prolonged arousal. Its hormone, when combined with epinephrine, has a similar synergistic (or permissive) effect, particularly on the heart and circulatory system. In addition, it increases the generation of heat from an overall increase in cell metabolism. It, too, requires hours or days in order to exert its effect.

It is the pituitary gland, which sits within the skull, that mediates the activation of the adrenal cortex and the thyroid, not the sympathetic system. (The pituitary and its control, the hypothalamus, are part of the limbic system, which appears to be the coordinating center of the authonomic nervous system.) Pituitary function is related to brain function (the central nervous system), and the pituitary gland is developmentally an outgrowth of brain tissue which has adapted to secreting hormones. It can secrete several different hormones, one of which, ACTH (the adrenocorticotrophic hormone), circulates in the bloodstream and specifically stimulates the adrenal cortex to create and release cortisone. Another, TSH (the thyroid-stimulating hormone), has a specific, activating effect on the thyroid gland. Other hormones released from the pituitary gland regulate such activities as sex gland functioning, bone growth, water balance in the body and mild secretion from the breast, but they do not play as prominent a role in the body's protective responses to environmental threat as do ACTH and TSH.

In summary, then, stress is usually defined as the activation of the arousal mechanism, especially the alarm mechanism defined as fight-or-flight. This physiological response to the perception of threat is mediated by the peripheral nervous systems—by the sensory-motor system and the sympathetic arm of the autonomic nervous system in particular. Also involved are parts of the glandular system which become more involved as the arousal continues over any length of time. It must be clear, then, that continued activation of sympathetic arousal can be destructive. We can literally wear our bodies out from it. This is what happens when the arousal pattern is sustained. This is what leads to stress—and this in turn leads to the breakdown of some physiological system. What is more, these prolonged states of arousal can lead to the depletion of reserves, which is called exhaustion. And this in turn leads to underaction, or an inadequate response to threats and dangers. It eventually leads to illness, defeat or death. So periodic relief from sustained sympathetic and hormonal activation is necessary for the repletion of glandular and fuel reserves; it is vital in preventing potential illness or death.

There are many techniques to reduce physical and mental tension and create a state of relaxation, most of which foster increased parasympathetic activity. But part of what actually happens when we relax may not be so much the result of an increase in parasympathetic activity as simply a decrease in sympathetic function. (Because the two systems often work to create opposite bodily effects, either a reduction in sympathetic activity or an increase in parasympathetic activity may result in the same physiological change.)

This can be most clearly seen in heart rate changes. For example, when one is exercising, the initial increase in heart rate comes about primarily from decreased parasympathetic discharge through the vagus nerve. In animal studies, this predominates until the heart rates reach 120 to 140 beats per minute. Then, if the exercise continues and becomes more strenuous (requiring an even faster heartbeat) the sympathetic system increases its discharge and the heart rate increases as a response. The phase of relaxation following exertion reverses the above process. First there is a decrease in sympathetic discharge; this is followed by an increase in parasympathetic dominance—although both systems continue to operate to some degree at all times. As stated earlier, the resting heartbeat represents a balance between sympathetic and parasympathetic activity.

What appears to be important to our physiological

functioning is an optimum balance point. It is well established that sustained or intense sympathetic dominance is very stressful and can lead to exhaustion, pathology and even death. By the same token, if there is sustained or intense parasympathetic activity, does this too lead to difficulties and physiological breakdown? The answer appears to be, Yes. Overreaction of the parasympathetic nervous system does appear to lead to pathology. Strangely enough, however, very little attention has been given to this area of study.

Although the subject is not well-understood, there are certain illnesses which appear to be associated with abnormal parasympathetic activity. An example of this is asthma, in which the airways in the lungs constrict abnormally and obstruct the smooth flow of air. Another is the duodenal ulcer, which results from an oversecretion of hydrochloric acid in the stomach. Both of these illnesses involve physical changes associated with increased right vagus nerve activity— and the right vagus is the major parasympathetic nerve.

There are other interesting events which point to the possible negative effect of excessive parasympathetic activity. Fainting from pain or from the sight of something repulsive takes place because of a strong right vagus nerve discharge to the heart which slows the pulse so much that the brain does not receive enough blood to maintain alertness. Oddly enough, the initial response to the anticipation of pain (as when one faces dental procedure) often involves the heart rate's slowing down rather than speeding up, indicating increased parasympathetic activity and predominance—even in the face of an overall increase in sympathetic function.

So it appears as if there are two possible responses to discomfort or to a perceived threat in the environment.

Along with (or even as an alternative to) an overall increase in sympathetic response, particular facets of the parasympathetic system may also become strongly activated and even override the sympathetic influence in specific areas of the body.

In addition, just as there can be abnormal overactivation of certain specific organ centers of the parasympathetic system (leading to reduced function and pathology), there also seems to be a general response pattern which may be termed excessive inhibition. This appears to be excessive generalized dominance of the parasympathetic system, which might manifest itself as pathological depression. (Remember that sympathetic discharge leads to arousal while parasympathetic discharge leads to inhibition.)

While it is clear that excessive sympathetic arousal can burn one out, excessive parasympathetic inhibition can be equally dangerous. For example, recent medical research has shown that there is a definite and well-established relationship between depression and certain forms of cancer. Depression has also been associated with a variety of psychosomatic diseases. While the exact mechanisms are not yet clear, it is known that those who undergo severe trauma from loss (such as the death of a spouse, or sometimes even retirement) may become so severely depressed that their death occurs within a relatively short period of time. The phrase, "He died of a broken heart" may be trite, but it does reflect a general awareness of the impact of grief, loss and depression on human functioning.

It is reasonable to assume, then, that when one consistently depresses (or excessively and constantly inhibits) one's internal systems, they begin to lose their capacity to function properly over a period of time. This would affect all internal systems, including the immune system, and there is a general recognition that it is probably the failure of this system which allows at least certain forms of cancer to develop. Thus, the relationship between depression and cancer begins to make sense.

The Possum Response

If we recognize that there can be a pathological over-dominance of parasympathetic activity (as well as of sympathetic activity), then we must reformulate our concepts of stress. It now appears likely that there is another pattern of responding (an adaptation pattern) that one may resort to when faced with what he perceives as a threat in the environment. Even though the traditional fight-or-flight alarm response theory (and actually Dr. Selye's entire General Adaptation Syndrome) is based on sympathetic arousal, there are a significant number of people who respond to threat with passive withdrawal, or what may be called the possum response. That is, instead of preparing to fight or run away when faced with a threatening situation, they just sort of roll over and play dead. Their response to fear is not arousal, but inhibition. This is marked by the typical characteristics of extreme parasympathetic discharge—decreased physiological functioning, loss of skeletal tone, mental lassitude, inactivity, and eventual depression.

The possum response is far too complex and extensive to be explained merely as an extreme state of flight. Nothing less than a General Inhibition Syndrome will explain the patterns and consequences involved when this passive response is activated. For example, in the fatigue stage of Dr. Selye's General Adaptation Syndrome, one's reserves are depleted. In depression, reserves are not depleted; they are simply not utilized. This is a different problem altogether!

The possum response may be originally rooted in the failure of autonomic arousal to adequately cope with what was perceived as environmental threats or demands, and it may have developed as a counterattempt to control them. It may also be a learned response developed from the socialization processes in which social dominance/submission issues were important determinents. In *Helplessness*, for instance, Dr. Martin Seligman shows how depression stems from learning the feeling of helplessness, and that this feeling can and often does lead to disease in the body and mind. What is more, it can ultimately result in death. It is more than likely that the possum response is a complex syndrome involving not only constitutional predisposition and socialization, but also the learning processes. In any event, it is evident that a number of people react to a threat by what can only be understood as parasympathetic dominance.

A Question of Balance

What makes an event stressful (excessive sympathetic or parasympathetic stimulation) in a harmful sense, or what leads to a state of balanced autonomic functioning has not been clearly understood. We all realize that someone can "worry himself to death," or "die of a broken heart" and even "die of joy," but no one has ever been accused of dying from tranquility or balance. While certain physiological weaknesses, such as a bad heart, can result in our being warned not to get too much excitement, we know that challenges, laughter and happy surprises are extremely beneficial to one's mental and physical well-being—yet all of these involve high states of arousal which, if sustained, become stress—and is dangerous. It is also obvious that relaxation is not only very pleasant, but extremely beneficial and very necessary. Yet very few who suffer from pathological depression would benefit from relaxation therapy.

With this in mind, we can begin to look at stress from a more comprehensive, and more functionally useful, viewpoint: *stress is a state of internal imbalance, reflecting the unrelieved dominance of either arousal or inhibition. This leads to impaired (damaged, or diminished) physiological and/or mental functioning.* Prolonged stress is a consistent pattern of imbalance (stress) resulting from the habitual dominance of sympathetic (fight-or-flight response) or parasympathetic (possum response) activity either in specific organ sites or as a generalized response pattern.

In other words, stress occurs when we are out of balance. This is illustrated in Figure 11 below. If we use the letter A, for autonomic, as a balance point, it becomes easy to understand the principle involved. The autonomic system is comprised of two cooperative arms, the sympathetic and parasympathetic systems.

Healthy, nonstress functioning is represented by a balance between the two sides. This can take the form of a dynamic balance, constantly adjusting back and forth in seesaw fashion as required to satisfy one's needs, as is represented by the dotted lines in Figure 11. As long as the pattern in activity remains balanced, (shifting back and forth in a fluid or dynamic pattern) there is no stress. Consequently,

Figure 11

Balance and the Autonomic Nervous System

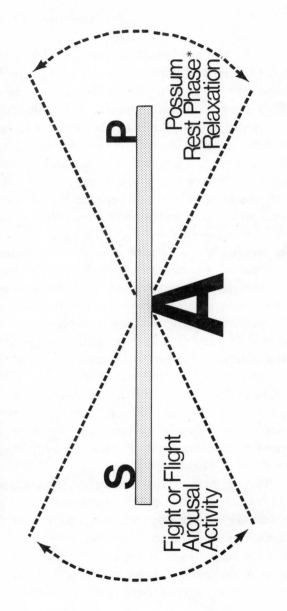

S — Fight or Flight Arousal Activity

P — Possum Rest Phase* Relaxation

(Regeneration, Inhibition)*

we can have periods of arousal (or activity) which are healthy and nonstressful as long as they are balanced by periods of inhibition (or relaxation and rest). In the same vein, a state of inhibition if it is not balanced by activity, can also become dysfunctional, resulting in lethargy and depression.

Balance may also occur at the point of homeostasis (or equilibrium) between the two divisions, as represented by the solid line in Figure 11. At this point the body is relaxed but the mind is alert. This is a very healthy state in which there is no stress (although a great deal of physical and mental activity can be accomplished while one is in it). Equilibrium in this case is reflected by the resting heartbeat (which is perfectly in balance but still accomplishing its job). A more complex example of this homeostasis is the meditative state of mind in which one is mentally very alert, but the body very relaxed.

We must keep in mind that Figure 11 oversimplifies an extremely complex system. Stress, or imbalance, can occur in many different ways, but whatever the particular pattern, if we have prolonged or intense parasympathetic imbalance we may develop the diseases associated with that imbalance (such as asthma or depression). If we have prolonged or intense sympathetic imbalance we may develop the diseases associated with that imbalance (such as coronary-vascular disease).

There are probably optimum balance points of organs, for systems (involving many organs), or even a generalized optimum balance point. And knowing this, we must recognize that all our organs and systems are interconnected. If an imbalance occurs within one organ, it will affect the rest of the system. Conversely, if the overall autonomic response is balanced, individual subsystems will begin to achieve balance.

If we understand stress to be a state of autonomic imbalance, then, we can eliminate the confusion between "good" and "bad" stress (which is really a confusion created by equating arousal and stress). The fact that we have either arousal or inhibition does not, in and of itself, mean we have stress. It is only when arousal is not balanced with relaxation or when relaxation is not balanced by activity, that stress occurs. So we have finally formulated a basic framework for understanding stress: *the key element in defining stress is whether or not there exists a balance, either dynamically or homeostatically, between sympathetic and parasympathetic activity.*

In other words, the principle is simple and clear; if you maintain neurological balance, you remain free of stress. On the other hand, anything you do can be stressful if you are out of balance. Thus, things or events which are stressful one day can be nonstressful the next. So the problem becomes one of learning to understand that which regulates autonomic functioning—the mind and its tool, the central nervous system.

The Mind and Stress

The most powerful source of stress is our own mind. Literally speaking, the central nervous system is ultimately responsible for initiating and orchestrating the responses of the peripheral nervous system, both the voluntary and the autonomic nervous systems and the glandular systems—but it is our mind which directs and stimulates the central nervous system. So in order to understand how mental functioning creates stress, we must first understand the basic physiology of this system.

The Central Nervous System—Control Room for the Mind

The peripheral nervous system transmits information; the central nervous system (CNS) organizes and integrates information. Since the central nervous system includes both the spinal cord and the brain, one way in which this takes place is through the convergence of certain nerve fibers as they travel up the spinal cord to the brain. Thus, small, localized reflexes (such as the stretch reflex) that are low in the spinal cord become part of a more complex pattern of movement initiated from higher centers within the brain. For example, at the spinal level a hundred or more carefully sequenced nerve stimulations may be required to create the pattern that results in our being able to walk, but the nerves involved will associate in order to convey a pattern to higher centers in the brain. There, a single stimulus applied to the correct area is thought to recreate the entire complex motion as the impulse spreads into the spinal cord along specific nerve pathways and automatically activates the appropriate spinal nerves and their associated muscles. The higher one rises in the brain toward the cerebral cortex, the more integration can occur, and this allows more and more complex behavior to be elicited by stimulation of a single nerve or small groups of nerves.

As the spinal cord rises into the head it widens into a region called the brain stem which is divided into four parts, one resting on top of the other. In the lowest, the medulla oblongata which sits just above the spinal cord, the basic respiratory and cardiovascular reflexes are coordinated—as well as arousal, alertness and sleep. Above the medulla, in sequence, are the pons, the midbrain (or mesencephalon), and finally the thalamus. It is the thalamus which receives all the sensory input from the body (much of which comes to it from nerve fibers traveling in the spinal cord) and acts as a relay station for that information on its way to the cerebral cortex.

In front of and below the thalamus is the hypothalamus, a small protuberance of nerve tissue which is of critical

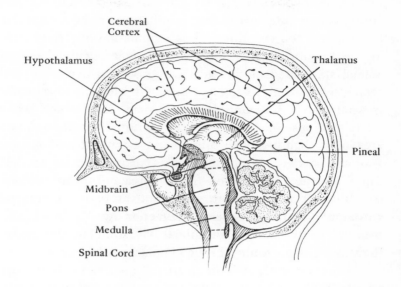

Cerebral Cortex

Hypothalamus

Thalamus

Pineal

Midbrain

Pons

Medulla

Spinal Cord

Figure 1
THE CENTRAL NERVOUS SYSTEM

importance in serving autonomic and other vegetative functions. Many small clusters of nerves, called nuclei, exist in this area, and strong experiences such as hunger, thirst, satiety, pleasure or pain can be felt when different nuclei are stimulated artificially (as can happen in brain surgery). One area of the hypothalamus, for instance, elicits a full coordinated discharge of the sympathetic nerves when it is stimulated, while a nearby area increases parasympathetic firing in the vagus nerves. The hypothalamus is also in direct contact with, and provides major control for, the pituitary gland.

The hypothalamus is also an integral part of the limbic system, the area of the brain thought to be responsible for instincts and emotions. Thus, stimulation of certain areas in the hypothalamus leads to a full rage reaction, and an animal stimulated in this area will growl, hiss, or spit—and attack immediately. Closely associated with the rage center is what is called a punishment (or pain) area, which, when stimulated, also leads to the rage reaction. Stimulation of an area only slightly above this creates a sensation of intense fear and anxiety, associated with a strong impulse to flee. The self-protective rage (or "fight") area and the nearby fear (or "flight") area are both strong activators of sympathetic autonomic discharge. Several millimeters away, however, is a pleasure center (which an animal will stimulate constantly if given the opportunity through implanted electrodes).

Consequently, within an area of the brain only the size of a large almond, nerve pathways involving intense emotional reflexes, pleasure and pain, autonomic functioning and hormone balance (via the pituitary gland) are all brought together. This takes place below the cerebral cortex region of the brain which is associated with voluntary action, self-control and what is considered to be self-awareness, or self-consciousness.

However, while much of the function of the hypothalamus appears to be involuntary and reflexive, there are many points of communication between it and the cerebral cortex. The relationship between mental activity (taking place within the cerebral cortex) and hypothalamic activation (such as occurs in a stress response) is extremely complex and not entirely understood, but studies conducted on animals provide us with some clues. It appears that new incoming sensory data (or experiences) will activate the cerebral cortex. If this and subsequent cortical activation is associated with activation of either the pain or pleasure center, the response in the cortex, along with the memory of the event, is reinforced and strengthened. However, if this experience is not associated with a parallel activation of either the reward/pleasure center or the pain/punishment center, the cortical response quickly disappears with subsequent repetition of the stimulus—and the events are ignored. (Incidentally, the pain response takes precedence over the pleasure response when both are stimulated equally.)

The Role of Cortical Events

While human beings are much more complex than animals, and our pains and pleasures much more intimately connected with belief systems (mental events) and habits, our physiological responses seem to be very similar in operation. It appears that when our experiences include a component of either actual or anticipated pain (based on memories of past similar experiences), they too can lead either to sympathetic or parasympathetic activity.

Whether we react with arousal or inhibition seems to depend on whether or not we perceive ourselves to be overwhelmed. If we can fight or run away, or if we are backed into a corner, we will respond with sympathetic arousal. If we perceive no hope, if we have the feeling that nothing we can do will help us, then we will tend to activate a possum response and become passive and depressed.

If the external stimulus is brief, and if we do not

extend activation in the cortex by ruminating on the threatening event, the associated autonomic response mediated in the hypothalamus will be brief. This might involve a mild increase in sympathetic discharge (with perhaps some increased adrenal hormone release) but without major activation of the emotions or the hormonal systems associated with the pituitary gland. In such a case, overall functioning can return very quickly to a balanced, relaxed state. If the external stimulus is persistent, however, and if cerebral activation is maintained because one cannot resolve a problem (or through persistent worry), then increasing degrees of sympathetic arousal can result which involve and reinforce greater degrees of emotional intensity. Then the pituitary, thyroid and adrenal cortex responses become involved.

If one has no awareness of this process, one is not able to allow the system to return to a balanced, regulated state, and then the stage is set for the appearance of stress. This is a crucial point. Stress may manifest either through the fight-or-flight response or the possum response, both of which are ultimately designed for self-protection. Both responses involve integrated cortical, hypothalamic, autonomic, neuromuscular and hormonal activity. Both are initiated, strengthened and maintained by our mental activity. Stress occurs when we do not understand the dynamics of the responses and when we do not recognize these responses when they are happening in us. We are thus unable to control, regulate and moderate the physical and mental activity of the fight-or-flight or the possum response from within.

The rudimentary connections of fight-or-flight are known, but the pathways of the possum response are not well understood. Either reaction, however, when not moderated and controlled, can lead to imbalance. This, in turn, can lead to increased susceptibility to illness, problems of depletion, inadequate tissue repair and healing as well as a decreased capacity for overall functioning.

Autonomic functioning is controlled mainly by the events that occur in the cerebral cortex, the part of the brain which organizes perceptual data and provides the context by which we interpret our world. *Thus, the primary source of stress is not the external environment; it is the emotional and perceptual factors which form our basic personality.* The greatest source of hypothalamic arousal comes from our own cerebral cortex in response to repetitive thought patterns, constant worries and apprehensions about unresolved past, present or future events which are associated with potentially painful or negative consequences in our lives.

Stress, then, is a physiological response to one's mental activities; it is the way we think about a situation that determines whether or not we will generate it.

Let us take an example of how we create our own stress. Remember when you were driving along a freeway on a Sunday afternoon. You had all the time in the world and were feeling content with yourself and everything else. Remember that you rarely had any difficulties with other drivers, and you were not even too disturbed by the occasional careless driver. Now compare this with the time you were angry with your spouse, late for an important appointment and needed to be across town ten minutes ago. At that time, wasn't every idiot in the world out on the freeway? But, do you honestly think that there is someone who runs up a flag that signals, "All idiots to the freeway!" whenever you get into your car and are in a bad mood—or in a hurry?

Of course not. Your world is a reflection of your mental state. The stress you felt on that trip was created by your own emotional processes. The idiots on the freeway are more or less constant in number, but your reaction to them varies. This depends upon the inner meaning you give to their actions.

In other words, your up-tightness is your own creation. You are not a helpless victim subject to the whims of fate; you can regulate your reactions to the situations you are involved in.

The biggest reason for our failure to deal adequately with stress is that we have been looking in the wrong direction. We have been operating under the false assumption that stress is a result of adverse environmental factors, and we therefore expect to find the source of stress in organizational structures, in poor communication between people, in the educational system, or in a thousand and one other places. Consequently, we expect to eliminate stress by manipulating the environment, by manipulating reinforcement contingencies and by altering physical symptoms with drugs.

As a result, thousands of hours, millions of dollars, and who knows how much honest effort has been spent in order to understand and highlight those environmental situations which produce stress. Communication channels have been examined from all angles; we have developed a sophisticated knowledge of drugs and their effects on the body; we have analyzed personality traits; we have had sensitivity training and all kinds of psychotherapies. The list goes on and on.

Unfortunately, at the end of it all one has a heart attack at the age of forty, and all that information, all that psychotherapy, all those pills, have been of no avail. The enormous effort, expense and training one has gone through has done little to alleviate chronic stress and its consequences. And indications are that the symptoms of chronic stress are increasing, not decreasing. Learning how to make our environment more peaceful for ourselves is certainly not a futile or useless practice, but it does not solve the major problem— our inner reactionary patterns.

If we really want to deal with our stress effectively, the first thing we must do is recognize that external events provide only the potential stimuli for change in stress levels. They do not actually produce stress, for this is done internally. When we realize this, we can consciously choose whether or not we do something about it.

Thinking and the Generation of Stress

Stress means that our mind is constantly creating problems and that we have developed both physical and mental habits which keep us from attaining balance. It means that we have either become accustomed to a state of constant low-level tension or that we have developed a withdrawn personality, sheltering ourselves from what the mind perceives as impossible demands. Neither manifestation is a "natural" state of being. None of us were born to be in a perpetual state of imbalance. To say that some personality types are more active and some are just naturally more passive than others is to beg the question, for within the framework of a general "type," we are all unique—and we can be balanced according to that uniqueness. We should not excuse a state of stress by saying, "Well, that's the way I am. There's nothing I can do about it." Stress is a condtioned state of being that can be altered.

We know that activation of the autonomic nervous system takes place when the organism perceives a threat in the environment. We know, too, that it does not matter whether or not this threat actually exists. The activating factor is one's internal (cortical) decision that a threat is there.

For example, there are many cases in which someone has robbed a bank, using only a toy pistol. The bank clerk, looking at the object in the robber's hand does not see the toy; he perceives a real pistol. Very quickly, and almost always unconsciously, the clerk anticipates the possible consequences (being shot, pain, and death), and the result is a strong activation of the fight-or-flight alerting mechanism or the possum response. In short, the clerk perceives a threat, becomes aroused (probably scared silly) and either faints or shovels the money toward the robber.

The clerk generated a stressful condition solely on a perception and the interpretation he gave to that perception. It is quite possible that the reverse could have happened. The robber could have used a real gun and the clerk could have perceived it as a toy and not reacted in a stressful manner at all. It is also possible that the clerk could have perceived that the gun was real but not responded with fear. So it is not only what we perceive that determines whether or not we activate an alarm response, it is also how we interpret the potential outcomes and the meaning of what we see. Thus, *stress is a direct consequence of how we define our personal relationship to the world!* The impact of a threat often continues long after the external event has actually passed. In fact, constant levels of stress are generated not by what is directly perceived, but by constantly ruminating on (or mentally reenacting) the sequence of events surrounding the threat. For example, our clerk may be terrified for weeks or months after the robbery, and by constantly brooding upon the sequence of events, he will be constantly setting off an alarm reaction, thus upsetting his autonomic balance. In short, we really do worry ourselves to death!

The "self" that may be threatened is not just the physical body; it includes anything to which one is emotionally attached—family, friends, automobiles, one's position at work or in the community, and even one's favorite football team. It is an emotional attachment that can best be understood as a process of identification with the object of attachment. In other words, the more I am emotionally involved with a person, object or idea, the more I am identified with it. Whatever threatens that person, object or idea will also hurt or threaten me, and the more identified I am, the stronger will be my response to the perceived threat.

Since it is our mental and perceptual responses (an activity of the cerebral cortex) that determine whether or not we experience stress, it is also here that we will find the key to mastering it—and all of our emotional responses as well. Think about this for a moment. We should realize by now that most of us have very little real control over the events in our lives. We buy insurance; we have pension plans and seniority; we develop special skills and abilities to insure that we will have work; we get married and have families so we will never be lonely. We take these actions and many more in an attempt to create some kind of order and control over our lives. And to some extent we succeed.

Yet we also recognize that at any time the world can run amok. Natural disaster, man-made calamities, accidents, divorces, change of bosses, someone changing his mind, stocks going down, the value of the dollar decreasing, all are beyond our control.

But if you can control how you *react* to all these things—what then? There is no way to control the world, but you can have control over yourself. You can control your reactions to the changing external events. You can learn not to be disturbed by whatever happens within and without. The problem now becomes, how do we become aware of these subtle mental processes that create such dysfunctional conditions for ourselves? We need to understand the process involved in creating stress.

We should begin with a working definition of emotional stress. That is: *emotional stress is the result of a mental process: It is a state of autonomic imbalance generated as a reaction to the perception of some kind of threat, pain or discomfort. This perception involves an interpretation of selected sensory stimuli, which is colored, or structured, by memories of past pain. It is also involved with the anticipation that this pain will occur in the future as a consequence of present sensory stimuli and environmental conditions. It is sustained by indecisiveness, the inability to resolve the threat.*

By the term *mental process* we mean that the major source of stress lies in our internal states. What happens is that by arbitrarily (but not necessarily consciously) paying attention to certain cues and not to other cues in our world, we, in a very real sense, program what we want our experiences of life to be. And when events do not meet our expectations, we often feel threatened, angry or disappointed —hence stress. Modern psychology has shown that we actively program our sensory equipment to pick up only what we believe, need, desire, fear, or have been conditioned to "see" (this is called selective perception). Our emotions and needs and past conditioning almost dictate how we use our sensory faculties. Furthermore, we organize new sensory input into categories which are based on our past learning (conditioning). So we tend to continually reinforce our original programming. In other words, we see the world as we have conditioned ourselves to see it. We are, however, usually not aware of the organizing facility of the mind (or filter mechanism), for it requires training in order to be able to attend to this process.

For example, if someone had a deck of cards on which the spades were red and the hearts were black, and if he flashed each card in front of us, we would probably see red hearts and black spades. When this experiment is actually done, many people are unable to change their conditioned mental categories, and this does not allow them to "see" what is really there. The same principle can also be seen at just about every sports event. The two groups of fans, one for each team, will generally have two differing views of what is going on. In a controversy, each will be absolutely sure that they knew what they saw! Still another example of preconditioning is when we believe that our colleague at the office is actively competing with us, when, in fact, he really isn't. We tend to ignore (or not perceive) those actions which are inconsistent with our beliefs, and interpret all others as proof of them.

What if our colleague really is competing with us? Do

we feel threatened, or insecure? Do we give it any importance at all? If we are secure and confident, we may be excited by it—or we may choose not to concern ourselves at all. On the other hand, if we interpret his actions as a possible threat, then we will react with anger, or aggression or fear. It is not the fact of what he does that matters; it is how and what we think about what he does.

In the same way, we create all of our fears (along with the other emotional disturbances which lead to stress). Self-deprecation, too, seems to be a major factor in creating autonomic imbalance, particularly on the parasympathetic side. For example, let us say that you knock over a glass of orange juice at the breakfast table. Your immediate mental response is, Oh, that was stupid. You have judged yourself harshly, perhaps out of anger or embarrassment—and you have also created stress. But all that was real was that the juice was spilled. The anger or shame or whatever that you felt was only the result of an interpretation you made of the event; it was not the event itself. The interpretation, however, has several important implications and consequences in terms of how you feel about yourself (and consequently, on your level of stress).

What goes through your mind when someone criticizes your work, or gives you a deadline that "must" be met? Are you aware of your own mental preoccupations when that happens, and are you aware of the consequences of those preoccupations? Most of us feel that we are usually pretty cool under pressure and fairly mature in our emotional responses. But the sad truth is that we are often woefully unaware of how our mind is shaping our reactions—unaware of how much time our mind spends in creating problems for us. The fears and punishments from which we suffer are usually not from life-threatening events, but rather from the petty little disturbances that we encounter on a day-to-day basis.

It would be impossible to catalogue all the fears that we suffer from. Fear of failure, rejection, of being "found out" are only the tip of the iceberg. Fears from financial pressures, time pressure, and deadlines are dangers of a more subtle kind. There are also fears of what others think about us, or our work, or our family. The fear of others' opinions, in fact, is probably the greatest "threat" that we have created for ourselves—with our negative self-judgments running a close second. These thoughts are so common and so subtle that we fail to recognize the tremendous pressures we are putting on ourselves to live up to some kind of perfection. Mistakes too often turn into convenient "whipping sticks" for self-flagellation, and we thus lose the benefit of the learning which always takes place when "mistakes" are made. All of these fears and judgments and many, many more create and maintain a constant state of stress in the body. The fact that we are insensitive to them does not eliminate them; it only allows them to operate unconsciously.

Inner Dialogue

Although most of us pay little attention to it, a continuous flow of mental activity containing a seemingly endless stream of thoughts, images, feelings and sensations is going on in our minds all the time. This can evolve into a kind of inner dialogue, and this is the stage at which we allow our mind to create stress. It takes place when we allow our thoughts to focus on fears, apprehensions, and judgments, and when our attention wanders off into past memories and/ or future fantasies. This activity is essentially useless—consisting as it does of endless speculations on future events (usually of the problem variety) and endless reconstruction of past events (usually of the "if only I had" variety). There is very little focus on the here and now. Unfortunately, most of us do this most of the time.

The first difficulty that arises from this inner dialogue is in its content, or what we think. That the cortical processes have the power to control physiological events has been well documented, but the implications of what this means have not been at all evaluated or understood. For example, we know that thoughts or images can create changes in the body. These may be as gentle as the slightly increased blood pressure and heart rate that take place when one thinks about doing exercise, and the increase of saliva in the mouth as one thinks about, or smells, food. More dramatic are the changes in physiology that are induced through hypnotic suggestion. Even more spectacular are the occasionally reported events in which some small woman has lifted an automobile off her child or husband who was crushed underneath, and those in which someone has carried a refrigerator out of a burning house single handedly. These situations indicate the power of cortical activity to initiate, direct and alter physiological events, through thoughts and images—and the more the emotional energy is tapped and directed, the more dramatic the event.

To demonstrate this for yourself, there is a small experiment you can try. Simply put your thumb and forefinger together, forming a circle. Have a very strong friend put his two forefingers through the circle of your thumb and forefinger, and, hooking his fingers around yours, ask him to try to pull your thumb and finger apart. At the same time, you try as hard as you can to keep him from pulling your thumb and finger apart. Of course your friend will succeed.

Relax your hand a minute or two and then try the experiment again. Only this time, close your eyes and picture, as clearly as you can, a large, beautiful monarch butterfly that you are holding between your thumb and forefinger. If you hold the butterfly too tight, you will crush its wings and kill it. If you don't hold it tight enough, the butterfly will flutter away. Thus, keep your arm, wrist and hand very relaxed, with just a very slight separation between the thumb and forefinger. When the image is very clear, nod your head and have your friend again try to separate your thumb and finger. No matter what happens, concentrate on holding the butterfly. Don't let go of it.

If you can maintain the image clearly in your mind, you will find that your friend will not be able to open your fingers. It would help if there were another friend standing there who would keep saying "Hold the butterfly, hold the butterfly!" This suggestion would help maintain and strengthen the image in your mind.

Now stop and think for a moment of the images and suggestions that you keep in your mind. Be particularly aware of those which are associated with a significant amount of emotional power. If you did the above experiment properly, you will have a better understanding of how the things that we think and imagine can have very strong effects on our body. If we think about (or imagine) that something terrible is going to happen, our whole body responds with arousal. If we constantly repeat negative thoughts, our body responds with depression. If we remember when someone cheated us, our body responds with anger and arousal. These kinds of cortical events are taking place constantly, and this is why our own thinking and imagining leads to emotional disturbance and stress. The power of cortical activity is the power of suggestion, and when we are constantly suggesting fears and negativity to ourselves, our poor bodies have no choice but to respond with stress.

It is not only what we think, but also the fact that we continue thinking it, that is important. Constantly repeating fearful or negative thoughts (such as worrying or brooding) maintains the alarm response. If we had a fearful thought or made some negative judgment, and let it go at that, the brief stimulus from the hypothalamus to the autonomic nervous system might result in some slight alarm response—but it would be brief and the body could quietly return to a balanced state.

When we constantly repeat the fearful or negative thoughts and images, however, it not only leads to greater neurological excitation, but it also activates the more prolonged stress response involving the endocrine mechanism as well. Thus our physiological response has become more involved, more pervasive and more destructive. The physiological response, in turn, stimulates more cortical activity, and a vicious cycle of self-suggestion and physiological activity ensues. The end result is a state of sustained imbalance, and eventually the breakdown of some system—and disease.

This constant repetition occurs because of indecisiveness—or the inability to decide what to do or how to handle the conflict in time, before the conflict or imagery has a chance to activate a more prolonged stress response. What allows for indecisiveness is a lack of will, or the ability to discriminate, decide and carry through with the decision. When a mental process involving some kind of anxiety is repeated over and over, a habit is formed which constantly creates stress. This further weakens the capacity of decisiveness, or will. Thus when we allow our inner dialogue to create an imbalance, we also hurt ourselves, through the weakening of our decisive faculty, by not resolving the imbalance. In this way stress leads to further stress.

This should give you an idea of how this inner dialogue can create problems for you. It happens because your autonomic nervous system does not conceptually differentiate between the past, present, and future. Whenever there is a thought in the mind, the nervous system responds to the action inherent in the imagery that thought evokes as if it were an actual event in the present and programs the body to perform an action in response to it. The more emotionally involved the thought, the greater the intensity of the body's involvement.

For example, if your attention wandered while you were reading this book and you thought of the gallon of milk you need to pick up at the store tomorrow, your body at that moment would be getting programmed to do the action inherent in that thought. But since most of us are not very emotionally attached to the act of buying milk, very little energy would be invested in that programming. Consequently, although the thought would create some very subtle changes in the breath and brain wave patterns, there would be little change in the body. If, on the other hand, you thought about your appointment with the IRS for a tax audit in two days, quite a lot of arousal would probably be programmed into the body. And if, at the time, you had been hooked up to some sensitive equipment that records physiological responses (equipment such as a brain wave machine, or an instrument that measures your muscle tension), technicians would have been able to measure some rather remarkable changes going on. This is all from the arousal mechanism responding to the presence of certain mental images having high emotional content.

Thus, as the flow of images and feelings wander in and out of thoughts of future and past events, the body is continually being programmed to perform actions. However, actions programmed from this imagery cannot be acted upon by the body in the present. You can imagine yourself striking back at someone, physically or verbally, for instance, but unless the person you are thinking about is there, or unless an opportunity arises to allow that action to take place, the programming cannot be completed, and the energy generated by the image of striking back cannot be expressed. Consequently, it remains locked in the body as tension and results in stress. This inability to express the actions programmed by mental imagery (or lack of coordination between body, mind and action) is a major factor in generating autonomic imbalance.

For example, there are many instances in which one is unable to express anger. It may be that he feels it is inappropriate, or he may be ashamed of being angry and think that it is not justified. The reasons for this may not even be conscious. They may be attitudes shaped long ago in his childhood. Whatever the reason, instead of being able to clearly say, "I am angry" or to somehow appropriately express the anger openly, he smiles or goes about his work with no apparent response. This results in stress.

Although we are seldom aware of the inner dialogue of the mind, just a little reflection will bring home its effects. We all know how an overactive mind can keep us from sleeping. It can also exhaust us. On the other hand, strenuous physical exercise or work can leave us tired but still feeling refreshed. We have all experienced those days when our mind is so completely absorbed in what we are doing that we forget all sense of time; we have been totally occupied with what we were doing at the moment. This might be chopping wood, playing handball, reading a book, drilling a tooth—or whatever. When it is over we may feel tired, but it is a very satisfying tiredness, for our chronic worries and cares have been totally set aside.

Compare this with the time you sat around all day worrying about something that was going to happen. You tried to work, but your mind kept going back to the same old groove; instead of concentrating, it ran here and there trying to figure out all the angles, reviewing all your mistakes and hurts. We have all felt that dragged-out, discouraged kind of weariness after a day of constant pressure and worry. Physical exercise and hard work leave the body tired, but the mind remains clear. The fatigue from mental strain leaves both mind and body tense and unfulfilled.

Mental fatigue is a consequence of where you focus your attention. When your mind is focused on the present, on the here and now, there is no conflict between mind, body and action. You become fully absorbed in what you are doing, whether it is planning the next advertising campaign, or working out a complex accounting problem, or deciding what the children should wear to school next year. Your focus of attention does not wander off, and your ability to work through problems is enhanced by the concentration. But when your mind wanders off into some past or future event, you lose the focus of your attention, and, through random associations, you may begin to create stress by anticipating some kind of problem. This is because our memory provides us with the ability to recall situations that created either physical or psychological pain, and remembering this pain we anticipate its recurrence in the future. Thus, through the anticipation of pain, or anxiety, or negative feedback, or social scorn, or disapproval, we activate an alarm mechanism and create stress in our minds and bodies. And this, of course, creates more problems for us—even to the extent of interfering with our ability to act or think at the moment.

The sex act, for instance, is very much related to the focus of attention. Generally the pleasure associated with it is intense enough so that all of our attention is focused on what we are doing. This enhances the pleasure, and we enjoy sex. However, we have all experienced sex when our attention was really on something else; we were preoccupied. At that time it was just so-so—pleasurable enough, but no great, intense event. In fact, one can even become so preoccupied that it is impossible to perform sex. Nearly all cases of male impotence, for example, are because of extreme preoccupation. For instance, if a man is afraid he cannot perform sexually (possibly because he is remembering his acute embarrassment when he failed the last time), his mind, focusing on the past event and apprehensive that it might take place again, actually brings that possibility to fruition—and sex becomes impossible. This is all because of the patterns of his inner dialogue and their effect on his body.

The martial arts give us a good example of how mental focusing on the here and now prevents anxiety and stress. They have as their main component a constant focus on the immediate present. There is no anticipation of what might happen, only full perceptiveness of what is happening now. And since there is no anticipation, there is no fear. Thus, there is no stress or tension to interfere with a creative and decisive response, with mind and body, to the immediate reality.

The Problem of Being Unconscious

Most of us pay little attention to our flow of thoughts, and we are often unaware when the fight-or-flight or possum response is operating. *The reason we suffer from stress is because we are insensitive to the mental and physical habits and patterns which maintain a constant level of activation in our bodies and minds!* Only when stress has reached the pain threshold do most of us allow ourselves to become aware of it. By then, however, it is too late to prevent the consequences. If you are sensitive to a particular emotional process before it becomes overwhelming, however, you have the opportunity to choose whether or not to take the steps necessary to rechannel the energy into more helpful and satisfying patterns.

This will be more clear if we use an analogy. Remember when you were a child running down a long hill? Remember how the momentum carried you along and how, at a certain point, it was almost impossible to stop? When I was a child I remember such a hill in an open field which we called the pasture. About two-thirds of the way down there was a ditch that you could not see from the top because of the long grass. In fact, you could not see the ditch at all until you were just a few feet from a drop-off into a large muddy area.

Well, we used to take friends from a different neighborhood to the top of the hill and shout, "Let's run down the hill! Last one down is a chicken!" With that, we would take off. By the time we were two feet from the ditch we were going pretty fast, and the poor kid from the other neighborhood would see it right in from of him. What was his reaction? Emotional conflict! He didn't want to run off the cliff into the muck, but he couldn't stop his body's momentum. Of course, since we knew where the ditch was, we could run right alongside of him and be prepared to veer off at the last minute—while he fell into the ditch.

This is analogous to what happens in our minds. We don't want to be angry, or fearful, but in some situations our emotions are strong, and by the time we feel or admit them, we are out of control. The emotional response is too much to direct. At best we can stifle it—but then we pay another price for the suppression or repression.

There is no denying the power of our emotional habits to create stress, but unfortunately very few of us have systematically developed our internal awareness to the point at which we are free from these subtle processes. However, increasing one's direct perceptual, or experiential, awareness leads naturally to a greater degree of choice and control. As we discovered in our childhood, if we can see the ditch from the top of the hill, we can easily direct our motion (energy) so that there will be no conflict.

Let us try an experiment. Stop reading for a moment and sit very quietly with your eyes closed. Now direct your attention to your body and its muscle structures. Are your jaws clenched? Do you feel any tension in the back of your neck and down into your shoulders? Are your leg muscles tense or jumpy? Do your eyelids flutter?

Even when you are doing something often thought to be relaxing, such as reading, you will retain tension because of the conditioned habits of your body—particularly in your muscles. And once the systems of your body become habituated to this, they have strong tendencies to retain the stress-reactive pattern even though the original stimulus is no longer there. Even more subtle are the persistent emotional patterns in the subconscious that are constantly programming the body to be tense. And once the body becomes habituated to a stress pattern, it will continue to repeat that pattern until one that is more helpful has been used consistently enough to replace it. The same is true of the emotional patterns in the subconscious.

We can train ourselves to choose our actions and responses, however, rather than reacting from past conditioning, and for most of us psychotherapy and depth analysis is not needed. While it is true that our fears, anxieties, negative judgments, anger and other such problems are rooted in our unconscious, it is possible to slowly bring them into direct conscious experience, ourselves. Gently confronting them will lead to conscious control. We all have the innate capacity to do this.

By understanding the role of the "attention" faculty of the mind, we can learn to use arousal and inhibition positively. Then, when we become absorbed in the immediate task, when all of our attention is focused, our concentration prevents mental wandering, and little or no attention can then be given to anticipatory thought patterns or memories. Consequently, there are no conflicting signals going to the body telling it to prepare itself to take actions which are incompatible with the present situation—and thus impossible to fulfill. If the present task results in a stressful condition, awareness of that condition is immediate, allowing one to respond appropriately to that stimulus and then regain his balance.

Thus, when we accept some challenge such as a task in which there is the possibility of failure, the mind does not focus on that possibility; it focuses on the task at hand. Then, even though the body may be under a strain for a period of time (such as when playing handball or having sex), the completion of the task signals the end of the arousal mechanism, and the body is then allowed to relax because the mind is relaxing. The challenge has been met, the actions taken, and the consequences (success or failure) are accepted, noted down for future reference and "forgotten." The attention is then focused on the next task at hand which more than likely will provide rest for the mind and body.

Thus, if one focuses one's attention on the immediate task, the autonomic system is not kept in a state of imbalance. The demands placed upon the body by the mental imagery are compatible with its opportunity to express them, and autonomic rhythm is not disrupted. Action programming is in tune with the physical situation, and this allows for a full expression of one's energy as well as a balanced coordination between mind, body and action. This attentive coordination allows the positive utilization of sympathetic (arousal) or parasympathetic (inhibition) dominance.

Another way to avoid stress is to achieve a homeostatic balance between sympathetic and parasympathetic activity. This can take place when one refrains from making any judgmental response to, or about, his perceptions and pays attention only to the flow of consciousness; when this takes place, the idea of having to think about what is happening is suspended; one simply pays attention to, or becomes a witness to, both internal mental/perceptual processes and external events. In other words one moves away from a categorizing, reactive, intellectualizing mode of being, to a pristine, perceptual mode of being.

This state eliminates excessive mental programming going to the body and results in a decrease in bodily tension—but at the same time there is no demand for excessive inhibition. Consequently, the sympathetic and parasympathetic systems achieve what appears to be a resting homeostasis (or equilibrium) similar to, and as balanced as, the resting heartbeat. This state is characterized by increased perceptual awareness without the added burden of increased physiological arousal. It is, unfortunately, rarely found in our society—but it can be achieved. Practical training can develop this skill, as we shall discuss in later chapters.

What is important to remember now is that we do have the power to control our minds if we become aware of what we are doing to ourselves. The next step is to increase our understanding of the mental/emotional, physical and behavioral habits which have their roots in the unconscious, for it is here that we must obtain our mastery over stress.

Our Habits and Prolonged Stress

As we have seen, prolonged stress is a chronic neurological imbalance maintained by our behavioral, physiological and mental habits. It is a constant level of stress that stems from an untrained mind which has not developed the power and habit of decisiveness, and as a result, it retains inner conflict and maintains a constant condition of stress, or imbalance. When one repeats a particular action over and over, one that is associated with some kind of anxiety, then he creates a habit which is a source of constant stress. This in turn can lead to the feeling that one is out of control, to a lack of self-confidence and eventually to the acceptance of stress as a "normal" part of living. This "helplessness" is a major component of prolonged stress. We adapt to the stress, accept it as a necessary evil—and the stage is set for disease.

Preliminary work by Dr. John Harvey at the University of Nebraska Medical Center, and continued at the Himalayan Institute, provides us with an example of how those who maintain constant levels of stress react. In his research Dr. Harvey presented the subjects with stressful tasks, such as mathematics, alternated with periods of rest. The subjects were attached to biofeedback machines, and during this time, Dr. Harvey continuously measured changes in their muscular tension in the forehead muscles (a good indicator of the tension in all the facial muscles) as well as changes in fingertip skin temperature. Muscle tension is an index of voluntary muscular activity, while fingertip skin temperature is an index of sympathetic (arousal) versus parasympathetic activity (relaxation). The colder the fingertip skin temperature, the greater the sympathetic activity (this is a general indication of increased arousal).

The research identified three kinds of subjects—those who sustained constant stress of the arousal variety, those who sustained constant stress of the inhibition variety and those who were able to relax and control their responses. Those in the first two groups all reported a variety of stress-related symptoms such as headaches, depression, insomnia and digestive problems. In Figure 1 below, the dotted line represents the typical response pattern of those who were found to have prolonged stress of the sympathetic variety (fight-or-flight arousal); the solid line represents the typical response of those who reported very few stress symptoms and who apparently coped well with stress; the broken line represents the typical response of those who were found to have prolonged stress of the parasympathetic variety (possum response—inhibition) and were also found to be withdrawn and depressed.

Those who had prolonged stress of the arousal variety began with higher levels of muscular tension and cooler

Figure 1
MUSCULAR AND VASCULAR RESPONSE PATTERNS
SHOWING THE EFFECTS OF PROLONGED STRESS

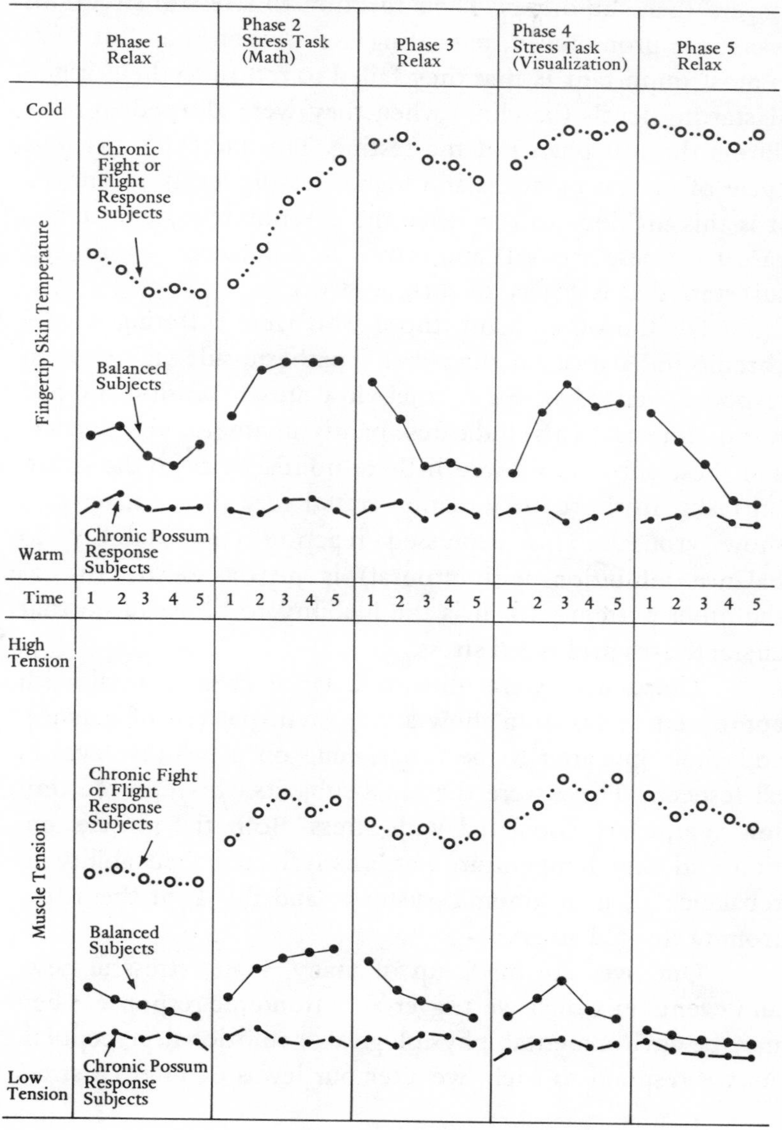

fingers than the others. Their reaction to stressful situations was more pronounced, indicating excessive arousal. But what is most important is that they failed to return to their original starting levels (baseline) when they were allowed to relax during the rest phases of the testing. This indicates a vicious cycle of increasing stress and higher resting levels of tension. It is this inability to rebalance the autonomic system (in this case to release arousal) and return to a balanced (more restful) state that is crucial in chronic stress.

On the other hand, those who were suffering from a chronic imbalance on the parasympathetic side (the possum response) started with extremely low muscle tension and had warm fingers. This indicates parasympathetic dominance, and these subjects showed little or no reactivity to the stressful tasks. In short, they demonstrated very little capacity to show arousal. This depressed reaction (the inability to balance inhibition with arousal) is just as destructive as the other extreme, for it is the inability to be balanced that characterizes prolonged stress.

Those who were able to balance their arousal with appropriate relaxation show a consistent pattern of balance, and they appeared to be functioning on a healthy level in all respects. These were the same subjects who reported very few symptoms associated with stress. Both the muscle tension and skin temperature patterns reflected their ability to rebalance their autonomic systems, and this kept them free from prolonged stress.

Our lives are made up of many, many stressful tasks and events in which we trigger an autonomic response. They may be environmental, physiological or emotional/perceptual. As we respond to each, we alter our levels of internal stress which is always shifting upwards or downwards, depending on how we are handling our affairs. If we fail to rebalance our systems, we begin to suffer from prolonged stress at that point. We then become accustomed to higher and higher levels of arousal, or to depressed functioning—and the trap is set.

Thus, the most destructive kind of stress is not an abrupt change in stress level—it is the daily wear and tear on our body that is sustained by our habit patterns because we remain unaware of (and consequently fail to rebalance) our autonomic responses. It is true that stress is most often created by the way we define, perceive and interpret our personal relationship to the world, but this process is based on habit—and we maintain stress by habit. So in order to understand, control and eliminate prolonged stress, it is necessary to become aware of and alter the behavioral, physiological and mental habits which sustain it.

Habit—The Unconscious Organization of Behavior

Man has long recognized that he is a creature of habit and that his behavior is conditioned and shaped by pleasure and pain. He thus seeks out that which is pleasurable and avoids that which is painful, and in so doing he develops habits. In the past fifty years or so the development of the behavioral sciences has led to the systematic explication of many principles and laws that govern habit formation (or behavior). We know, for instance, that certain patterns (called schedules) of positive reinforcement (reward, or pleasure) will elicit very strong and consistent patterns of behavior. We know too that other schedules of positive reinforcement will shape or condition patterns of behavior that will not be as strongly consistent, or that can be easily deconditioned.

For our purpose here it is not necessary to repeat and summarize the findings or philosophy of Behaviorism. We need only to understand on a practical level what habits are, how they operate and affect us, and what we can do to bring the powerful tool of habit formation under our conscious control. In short, we need to understand how to use the power of habit formation in a more skillful way.

We can understand that habit is a very purposeful behavior which is organized (shaped, conditioned) to exist within certain consistent parameters and in such a way as to operate efficiently without the necessity of conscious control. Habits are shaped (organized) through a process of conditioning (learning), whether conscious (as in learning how to drive a car) or unconscious (as are the bulk of our emotional and attitudinal habits). The latter are largely shaped by parents and society. In yoga psychology this process is also understood, but it is taken to more subtle levels. For instance, pain and pleasure, the controlling elements in the formation of habits, are seen to arise out of the contact of the senses with the sense objects. Thus the interaction of inner sensory abilities plays an important role in determining habits as well as controlling them.

Habit formation is a very powerful tool of the mind. In and of itself, it is neither good nor bad, but like our tool of vision or our ability to use our hands and fingers, the ability to form habits can lead to either positive results (such as good driving habits) or harmful results (such as smoking). Nearly everything we do, think, feel and perceive is either influenced or controlled by our habits. Another way of saying this is that we are a product of our conditioning.

So strong is this conditioning, that our internal behavior is guided by habit as well as our personality traits and eccentricities, for emotional habits lead to biochemical and structural habits in our internal organs and musculature. For example, habits of posture influence our habits of attitudes and vice-versa. (*Bodymind*, by Ken Dychtwald, gives a thorough discussion of this relationship.) In addition, our habits interact with each other to provide consistent patterns of behavior, with consistent outcomes, and this reinforces further habitual behavior. In other words, we go through our daily activities operating primarily, if not exclusively, on habit.

What we eat, when we eat and how we eat are determined by habit. All of our skills—typing, playing handball, management, fire-building—are determined and controlled by habit. Sexual activity is controlled by habit. The friends we choose, the work we do, the clothes we wear are all controlled by habit. Of course there are other factors involved in our behavior. Our constitutional make-up and our environmental surroundings provide the basic potentials for, and often the limits of, what we can do. (No matter how hard we practice, for instance, we will very probably never be able to fly by merely flapping our arms.)

But the tool of habit formation is nevertheless a pervasive and powerful determinant in our lives and can be very useful. Habits minimize the amount of effort required to do a task; habits structure internal and external environments and provide stability; habits allow for an orderly and efficient progression of daily activities; habits allow us to live skillfully and usefully. Habits can also kill us.

We are all aware that we develop habits which can and do have serious consequences. Taking drugs, bad driving habits and poor dietary habits are only a few of the more obvious ones. Psychotherapists work with attitudinal, emotional and behavioral habits which lead to anxiety and depression. Dentists must deal with the ravages of poor dental and dietary habits. Doctors attempt to alleviate the symptoms of poor health habits. Nearly everyone suffers from the habits which result in prolonged stress. Thus, knowing that habits may be either useful or damaging, we must learn how to bring the power underlying habit formation under control and eliminate those which create problems for us.

The Unconscious—Home of the Habit

The purpose of habits is to allow us to develop skills which can operate at an unconscious level (unconscious refers to anything that is not directly conscious, including the subconscious). Thus our minds are free to concentrate on more important activities and we can focus our attention without needing to attend to those things which can be done habitually.

The principles and laws which govern the activation of habit patterns have been systematically explicated by Pavlov, Skinner and others, but they apply to behavior only as long as it remains on the unconscious level. Thus, whatever environmental conditions serve as a stimulus to (or reinforcement contingency for) a particular habit response will control the activation of that response in the unconscious. When a behavior pattern (or habit) is controlled by an environmental stimulus, the individual controlled by the habit is also controlled by the environmental stimulus (reinforcement paradigm, or pain and pleasure).

For example, you may have acquired the deep-seated habit of feeling incompetent. This attitude, learned as a child, lies in the unconscious, and you are not fully aware of this quirk in your makeup. However, whenever someone questions your judgment, you react with anger or aggression, overwhelming your questioner with logical and often intense argument. This intensity does not make sense until one realizes that what is really happening is that the feeling of incompetency colors the perceptual response, and you perceive a threat when none was intended. This, of course, stimulates autonomic arousal, and you, the "threatened" one, reinforce your constant level of stress—never aware of the real reason behind your actions.

Emotional habits in the unconscious are thus the primary sources of stress, and we maintain this stress through all sorts of physical habits. Take, for example, those who gobble down their dinners in record time, meal after meal. The food is there, and the setting has become a stimulus for the habit of eating fast—even when there is no time pressure.

The body, too, develops habits which reside in the unconscious. Many tension headaches, for instance, are a result of chronic tension in the masseter (jaw) muscle. The psychological reasons behind the clenching of the jaw may have long since disappeared, but the habit of clenching still remains, continually creating muscle tension that eventually leads to headache. One becomes aware of the chronic tension only when pain has been created by the constant pressure, and then most people, although they feel the head pain, remain unaware of the tension in the jaw muscles.

Different habit patterns may operate as a result of entirely different reinforcement and stimulus conditions. They may have developed for completely different reasons, and they may have totally different psychological involvements, but they do share one thing: they operate in, and because of, the unconscious mind. And it is the unconscious mind that controls the conscious mind.

All habits and behavior can be controlled if one is fully aware of the patterns that are taking place, for habits control actions (behavior) only to the extent that they are allowed to operate at the unconscious level. As soon as one is conscious of his behavior, he can consciously choose not to act according to the old pattern instead of letting the habit automatically determine the behavior.

The awareness however, must be complete and constant. Partial awareness results in only partial control and often conflict, for the conscious part of the mind wants one behavior and the unconscious is programming a different behavior. Whichever has the highest emotional charge, or energy, is the one that usually determines the course of action. Only full awareness—direct experiential awareness and knowledge of the habit pattern—allows one to develop full control.

When a compulsive eater, for instance, becomes overly stressed, he will start snacking. The reason he gives for eating is that he is hungry, but that "hunger" is not really for food; it is the conditioned response to a high level of tension, and it temporarily reduces that level. Unfortunately, eating can never eliminate stress, for eating is actually a response to satisfy the stimulus of real hunger, or nutrient deprivation. On an unconscious level, however, suppressed feelings of another nature may be associated with eating. Repressed sexual urges, for instance, and the associated guilt, desires, and whatever else is a part of the complex, continue to create a disturbance—and, of course, a constant level of stress.

Let us say that our compulsive eater gains some awareness of his stress and becomes aware that he eats in order to reduce it. Being sensible, he decides to stop his compulsive stress-snacking. What then follows is a constant battle between his good intentions and will power, on the one hand, and his habits of snacking (which he is now becoming more and more conscious of), together with the suppressed sexual feelings (which he is not aware of), on the other.

Our compulsive eater has made an important beginning —but only a beginning, for he may continue to have conflicts until he has become conscious of the inner emotional quirk of suppressed sexual feelings and the constant stress resulting from this repression. In other words, he may have stopped his compulsive eating, but this has not given him freedom from the stress.

There are seemingly endless unconscious conflicts which can serve as sources of unrecognized stress, but unfortunately most of us do not develop the sensitivity necessary in order to be consciously aware of them. This is the primary reason we continue to suffer from prolonged stress. Our focus is on the external world in a vain attempt to control those conditions which are the stimuli to our habits, and our success is minimal at best. What is needed, however, is not to control the endless events in our environment. It is exactly the opposite. We need to control our responses to the environment. It is impossible to control the world. The only reality is change. How can you control that?

On the other hand, with proper self-training (and the expansion of our awareness), we can control and be responsible for our responses to whatever happens in the world. That is the key to eliminating stress. We must now understand how our habit patterns (which maintain stress) can be altered so that we can eliminate it.

The Habit of Prolonged Stress

Our mind, body and behavior are all functionally interrelated, constantly influencing one another—interacting in a dynamic process. We are not made up of isolated, mechanical pieces. We become hungry, and we eat. What we eat and how we eat has an effect on how we feel and think. Our posture reflects our mood and, in turn, influences it. If you want to experience this yourself, try walking around slump-shouldered for a few hours and see what happens to your mind.

There is always a complex, interdependent and interactive process that constitutes the totality of our being. So it is also with those habitual behaviors which are associated with stress. They reflect a stressful state, and they also reinforce and expand a stressful state. For example, we become tense, angry or frightened, and we tense up our neck and shoulder muscles. After this has happened thousands of times, the shoulder and neck muscles develop a habitual response, involving tension, and any stimulus, however slight, immediately sets off the habitual tension response in the musculature. As a consequence the neck and shoulder muscles remain constantly tense—not because one is necessarily always under a lot of pressure, but because the muscles have developed a habit. Furthermore, these muscles send signals back to the mind so that the body is prepared for action when, in fact, there is no action called for. The mind receives the message, "be prepared; something is going to happen." It perceives no danger, but there is still a feeling of apprehension.

By becoming aware of what we are doing when we are doing it, however, we have the opportunity to behave differently—to create a behavior keyed to relaxation rather than tension. For instance, we are not usually aware of tension in our shoulders (or in any muscles, for that matter) until there is stiffness or pain. By then it is too late to prevent the discomfort. If, on the other hand, we were sensitive to the muscles when they began to tense, we could immediately and easily take the action necessary to halt the process. Simply bringing our awareness to those muscles initiates a corrective response. Thus, *by increasing your sensitivity to stress-related behavior, you immediately begin to exercise greater control over it and alter it in a positive direction.*

Our ability to be conscious of and to consciously control our internal states as well as our external behavior is far greater than most of us have experienced, for our bodies have extremely sophisticated internal sensory mechanisms. For example, in classes in which one is taught to quiet the body and mind and begin to pay attention to what is going on internally, many students are amazed to hear how loud and strong their heartbeat is. It has always been that way. The student has simply to become conscious of it. We, too, must become sensitive to both internal and external patterns of behavior if we are to gain control over stress.

We can arbitrarily divide our habits into three areas of concern:

1. Behavioral habits: These are our characteristic behaviors such as our work habits, our eating and driving habits and our social habits. They are the external patterns of behavior.

2. Physiological habits: These are our internal physiological patterns such as our breathing habits, muscular habits, vascular habits and other consistent patterns of activity in our internal environment.

3. Mental habits: These are the emotional/perceptual habits which are also the creative sources of stress.

Behavior—The External Symptoms of Stress

Because of our lack of inner awareness, our overt behavior is often the first indication we have as to our level of stress. Behavior is something that everyone can see (a fact that is not lost to the behavioral psychologist), and thus it can be a standard by which to assess levels of stress. However, our external behavior is only the reflection of our inner state, not its cause. Merely changing it may not affect our level of stress.

It may be that one's behavior is empty of a driving (or compulsive) emotional force, since habits have the power to exist in and of their own structure. That is, a habit may not be, in itself, linked to an underlying conflict. In this case a change can be made effectively without concern for the underlying compulsion. However, it may also be that behavior is an expression (or release) of an inner compulsion or state of tension. In this case changing the behavior will not necessarily alter the compulsion; the change will only lead to another stress-related habit without having made any change in the internal state.

It is not the behavior that is the problem, it is the underlying constant level of stress that we are concerned about. Behavior is a result of an internal motivation that must be understood in order to resolve the stress.

It is important to understand that developing an awareness of overt behavior patterns is not just an exercise in counting stress symptoms. Becoming aware means that you are increasing your sensitivity to the actions you are performing and to the associated mental/emotional events which are also present.

How does this happen? When a habit associated with a certain level of stress is acted upon, it reinforces or strengthens the internal pattern of stress. Thus, behavior not only reflects stress, it also reinforces it and helps to maintain it chronically. By being aware of behavior as it is taking place, however, you immediately have the chance to stop the pattern. You can simply choose not to continue it. This choice, in itself, will at least not reinforce the internal compulsion. It can also give you an opportunity to focus your attention on the internal state and become aware of the cause/effect relationships between the two.

Then, by giving yourself the choice of whether or not you will continue the stress-behavior, you have given yourself the opportunity to consciously insert a relaxation response, or a behavior that is not stress-reinforcing. This not only weakens the habit strength of the stress-behavior, it also alters the internal level of stress.

For example, if I have a habit of eating when I become tense, I have several options. I can go along with (and continue) my habit (eating when I am tense and then suffering the consequences)—or I can substitute an alternative behavior. Let us assume that I am gaining weight, feeling guilty about all the snacks I take, and suffering the ups and downs associated with the drastic changes in blood sugar levels that take place when a person ingests a high sugar snack on a relatively empty stomach. My eating does nothing to alter the constant level of stress. In fact, my erratic and poor diet and my emotional ups and downs lead to even greater stress.

If, on the other hand, instead of eating I substitute a relaxation or breathing exercise, I not only reduce the compulsion to eat (which was really a thinly-disguised stress response and not really hunger), I also do not suffer from the consequences of the inappropriate eating. To be able to make this choice requires an awareness that the behavior is either taking place or is about to take place; it also enables me to consciously take alternative action. While I must become educated as to a more helpful behavior, the first step is to bring the habit of eating when I am under stress out from the unconscious mind by becoming aware of it. The more aware I am, the greater the opportunity for choices I have, and the more control I have over these behavior patterns.

It is important to understand that this choice must be made from one's own level of awareness. No one can be aware (or conscious) for another. It is ultimately his own responsibility (not to be confused with blame). If we choose not to be aware, no therapist, doctor, friend, spouse or even God himself can do that for us. And if we choose to remain insensitive, if we allow our habit patterns to remain in the unconscious, we can never alter them.

The list of symptoms given in the first chapter are typical indicators of stress, but it won't solve the problem. We can listen to our family and friends when they tell us that our actions reflect stress, but that won't teach us. If we really want to know if our behavior is stress-related, then we must pay attention to what we are doing and how we feel when we are doing it. In other words, we must become responsible for ourselves.

The Physiological Habits of Stress

The various physiological systems of the body are also subject to habit patterning. Our musculo-skeletal system, our glandular system, our digestive tract, our cardiovascular system, our organ systems are all subject to developing stress-related behaviors (or habits), and these are the foundations of many of our disease states, particularly psychosomatic diseases. When a stress-habit involves the vascular system, for example, we can gradually develop such problems as migraine headaches or Reynaud's Syndrome (a disease in which the peripheral blood vessels degenerate and the tips of the toes and fingers begin to rot because the cells are not receiving an adequate supply of blood), or we may develop "essential hypertension" (a habitual cardiovascular response to chronic stress, or stressful events).

Biofeedback provides an excellent example of how

increased awareness leads to greater control. As stated earlier, this is the use of some kind of instrument, usually electronic, which monitors a physiological process and then provides an ongoing feedback signal indicating what is happening in that process. A major area of focus is the EMG (electromyograph) biofeedback in which the electrical activity in a muscle is monitored and the signal tells one when the neurons in the muscles are firing and when they are not. In other words, the instrument directly reflects the level of electrical activity in the muscle, and by a signal that changes with the activity, it tells one what is going on inside the body at that moment. The more the electrical activity, the greater the degree of tension in the muscle.

But the biofeedback instrument only reflects one's internal state. It is a tool to help one to develop direct experiential awareness of previously unconscious internal processes, and when one becomes sensitive to the internal processes he very quickly develops conscious control over them. At this point, instead of letting the unconscious stress-related habit control (or elicit) the physiological response, one can alter and control that response and consciously train a new, more helpful, healthful habit pattern.

Research has clearly shown that those who were taught to focus their attention on the biofeedback signal were unable to control the target physiological response once they no longer had access to the equipment. In other words, since they developed no internal awareness of their physiological process, they were unable to maintain control over it. On the other hand, those who were trained to use the signal as a mirror to reflect their own internal processes, and who used that mirror to develop internal awareness or sensitivity to those events, were very quickly able to control the physio-logical process. In fact, after a short period the biofeedback equipment was not necessary. In many cases it actually interfered with internal concentration.

Biofeedback works because it allows one to become conscious of the control he already has over his physiological process. Thus he is able to modify, alter or change those controls to effect a more positive process. Through biofeed-back and more sophisticated internal tools (such as hatha yoga, breathing and meditation practices) we, too, can change unconscious stress-related physiological habit patterns to those which are more useful.

The belief that we cannot, and do not, control certain parts of our body is false. The truth is that we have absolute control over our body. The problem lies in whether or not it is conscious or unconscious. Unconscious control means habit—conscious control means choice!

Developing physical awareness is not only necessary in order to eliminate stress, it is often quite a lot of fun. As has been said, 'the key element is awareness—removing the habit pattern from the unconscious so that those which create stress can be altered. What you can do to develop this awareness will be discussed in the next chapters.

Mental Habits and Stress

The most difficult area to control is the mind; yet its habits are the controlling motivational forces behind nearly everything we do. The seat of our personality (or sense of I-ness), the mind, is profound in its capacity and depth, and to gain direct experiential awareness of its contents requires persistent effort and training. But it can be done.

Most of us are only superficially aware of our fears, desires, needs and wants. We do not know how to systematically expand our awareness into the areas of the subconscious and unconscious; we are often too much in awe of that part of the mind, for we have been taught that the only communication we can have with it is indirect communication through symbolic representation such as dreams and ink blot tests. We have been told that direct experiential knowledge of the unconscious may take place only after years of analysis, and then only with the help and guidance of an analyst. In fact, our supposed inability to directly confront our own unconscious states has been the basis for much of Western psychology and psychiatry, particularly Behaviorism.

What does not seem to be understood by most professionals and professors is that there is a definite methodology for systematically bringing the unconscious into consciousness. This is not a mystical or magical process; it is simply training the attentional faculties of the mind. It is training the inner concentration abilities; it is the ability to focus inwardly with detachment; it is a state of neutral observation. The mind thus becomes the object of consciousness. This process is called meditation.

There are many forms of meditation, and this subject will be discussed in a later chapter. It is enough to say here that mental states are no different from either physiological states or external behavior in the sense that they may become objects of consciousness. In other words, mental (emotional/logical/perceptual) phenomena need not remain in a subjective relationship to the observer; they can become objective realities by properly training oneself and establishing inner concentration.

As with stress-related physiological habits or external behavior, awareness of stress-related emotional/mental habits provides us with the immediate opportunity to act differently and to control the entire behavioral sequence through conscious choice.

Training in the Science of Awareness

The point of everything that has been discussed so far is that we suffer from prolonged stress primarily because of our habits, for the human personality is composed of various types of habits which govern our lives. After analyzing habit patterns, we come to know that habits have their basis in the unconscious mind, and that the unconscious mind controls our conscious activities. Thus we can come to understand our unconscious mind by becoming aware of, and directly experiencing, our habits. What allows these habits to continue to create and maintain constant stress is our lack of sensitivity to them and to their consequence. If we were fully conscious of how we created our own problems we would very quickly stop, for no one knowingly chooses to be in pain.

This principle is very well understood in the science of yoga in which it is recognized that suffering is the direct consequence of undifferentiated consciousness, or what in yoga is referred to as ignorance. This does not mean that we are stupid, or dumb; it means that we are not aware of our true nature. We ignore the inner reality, and thus we create stress! In other words, according to yoga we are unconscious of those mental/emotional/perceptual processes which habitually create stress. Most important, we are not aware of our true nature—pure consciousness or awareness—which is free from all suffering. As a result, we identify ourselves with objects or emotions that are part of our habit structure, and these are subject to both change and to threat. The consequence of this is constant stress, or suffering.

As a holistic science concerned with all aspects of human functioning, yoga science provides a unifying framework by which stress can be understood and eliminated. It involves a systematic method by which we can begin to expand our awareness of these processes and thus begin to gain control over them. So in a very practical sense yoga gives us the tools and techniques by which we can expand our conscious awareness into the unconscious parts of the mind in order to become aware of the patterns and habits which lead to stress.

In the next section, *Freedom,* we will deal with the skills necessary to gain freedom from stress. This will entail working with the whole person, as it is the whole person that is subject to habit. Sensitivity and awareness give us the power to free ourselves from stress, and they must be complete and constant. Superficial awareness gives superficial freedom—which means no freedom at all, for the pathway to freedom lies in our conscious power to maintain balance.

Freedom

Part Two

Diet and Exercise

Obviously, the health of our physical body is important to our survival, so we begin the path to freedom at this, the most basic level. Most of us are all too familiar with the signs and symptoms of structural (or bodily) stress. The symptoms may vary—tense neck and shoulder muscles, indigestion, cramps, awkwardness—but they all reflect habitual patterns of autonomic imbalance as it manifests itself in structural tension.

Most of the ways in which we deal with these symptoms give us only temporary relief. Hot baths, saunas, massage and whirlpool baths are all helpful. More sophisticated massage techniques such as a complete massage, Rolfing and *shiatsu* (an acupressure technique) are also therapeutic tools that can have beneficial effects on structural tension as well as emotional stress.

Helpful as they are, however, these techniques tend to be primarily palliative, providing only temporary relief.

It is true that massage may alter the structural condition of the stress pattern, but it rarely has any effect on altering the underlying physical/mental/emotional habit patterns. In other words, these techniques relieve stress, but they do not alter the stress syndrome. And eventually the symptom reappears. Our goal is not merely to relieve stress symptoms; it is also to alter (and gradually eliminate) the habits which led to them in the first place, and in order to accomplish this we must gain direct experiential awareness of these patterns and gradually reshape them. This requires self-awareness and self-regulation.

There are two major areas in which one can develop control over the habits of the body—diet and exercise. Both can be brought under one's own control, and both can lead to significant reductions in stress.

Diet and Stress

As a source of stress, a poor diet is second only to emotional (or mental) events. Given modern dietary habits, the simple fact that we eat several times a day is more than enough opportunity to generate constant imbalance. For the high and increasing incidence of "digestive diseases" (diseases of the gastro-intestinal tract) are ample evidence that, as Dr. Roger Williams states in *Nutrition Against Disease*, diet is a significant determinant of our health.

Recently the National Commission on Digestive Diseases released a comprehensive report; their findings include the following:

1. More people are hospitalized and more undergo

surgery for digestive diseases than any other.

2. Ten percent of all money spent on medical care is spent on digestive diseases.

3. In 1978 digestive diseases cost more money than cancer.

4. If deaths due to cancers of the digestive system are included, digestive diseases are the third leading cause of death in our society.

5. Digestive diseases are the second leading cause of worker disability and account for one of every six worker absences.

Experts in the field of nutrition all agree that American dietary habits are a national disaster. This means that modern man does not pay enough attention to the quality of the food he eats, nor does he eat it properly. He is not aware of the fact that food without nutritious value is unhealthy. He eats too fast; he has lost the art of cooking and preparing food; he has allowed junk food to dominate his diet. After becoming aware of our habits, however, we will find that bad dietary habits can create constant stress.

Serious observation shows us that there are two complementary dietary processes that go on in the human body— nourishing and cleansing. If we do not regulate them with proper dietary habits, the body gradually builds up toxins which are the basis for many mental and physical difficulties. So we must regulate the what, when and how of our diet in order to prevent our food from creating stress.

The Quality of the Food We Eat

Fresh, simple and nutritious are the food qualities most suitable for our health, but amazingly enough, fully sixty to seventy percent of the average American diet is of suboptimal nutritional value. This is not because there isn't enough to eat; it is because much of what we eat is not useful to us. Refined sugar, for instance, which contains absolutely no nutrients, makes up twenty-five percent of our diet, and fats, which also contain no nutrients, make up forty-five percent. This is seventy percent of our food.

Besides increasing one's nutrient debt, refined sugar is directly associated with serious physical dysfunctions such as obesity (a major disease in modern society). In addition, the precipitous rise and decline in blood sugar that results from the intake of refined sugar can lead to a strain on the liver as well as imbalances in insulin production. This in turn leads to both hypoglycemia and diabetes. A more serious consequence is the danger posed to the nervous system—such as a diabetic coma. Low blood sugar is also associated with psychological stress as manifested in anxiety and restlessness as well as tiredness and depression. Other dysfunctions related to high sugar intake are kidney irregularity, fluctuations in blood pressure, and the intensification of emotional imbalance.

It is true that sugar in the blood is the major fuel for our cells, but we can usually get enough naturally-occurring sugar in fresh fruits, vegetables and grains. It is important to be aware of this, for sugar in any form is a stimulant and leads to heightened arousal; refined sugar is too much of a stimulant for the body to be able to handle comfortably. For instance, when we are tired we traditionally "take a break" for coffee or something sweet—or both. Since these are stimulants and usually chock-full of refined sugar, there is a rush of sympathetic activity which is felt as a new burst of energy. This increased sympathetic discharge, which leads to increased autonomic imbalance (stress), leads to even more fatigue—particularly in those who suffer from low blood sugar. In other words the "relaxing" coffee break is actually a stress producer!

Far more appropriate, when one is tired, would be relaxation and/or breathing exercises. These lead to autonomic balance (and the reduction of stress) and are wonderfully refreshing as well. One's energy levels would then be appropriate to the tasks that needed to be done. One would be neither overstimulated nor depressed. Residual tension would not be robbing the body of energy. This kind of break would not result in even greater states of underlying fatigue, nor would it lead to the withdrawal problems associated with stimulants.

This does not necessarily mean that we should eliminate refined sugar—although this has been persuasively argued by many researchers. Instead, we should begin to be aware of how refined sugar may be creating serious problems for us as individuals. Certainly an average yearly consumption of about 125 pounds per person, twenty-five percent of the diet, is not intelligent.

Another forty-five percent of the average American diet is fats—which are also "empty" calories (they have no nutritional value). While a certain amount of fat is necessary (probably around ten percent of our total diet), it is quite destructive if it is almost half of our total food intake. Most knowledgeable medical authorities agree that a high-fat diet is associated with heart disease, and in *Diet and Nutrition* Dr. Rudolph Ballentine points out its correlation with cancer (particularly cancer of the colon).

Thus we can see that a major problem for modern man is that a great deal of what he eats not only fails to provide any nutrition but also leads to serious diseases. This cannot help but lead to serious autonomic imbalances—which is stress.

Other things that we ingest can also lead to serious stress problems. For instance, Americans yearly consume an estimated five pounds of chemicals which do not occur naturally in the food chain, for there are over 2,000 additives commonly used by the food industry. When taken individually or in combination, and subjected to the refining process called digestion, the consequences are not well known. Add to this combination the herbicides and pesticides which enter the food chain, and we are looking at a chemical mixture that is potentially dangerous. Its long-term effects on such delicate mechanisms as, for example, genetic structures over generations, is largely unknown, and to assume that it is safe to take this mixture into our bodies is more than naive; it is foolhardy. Chemicals which do not occur naturally in the food chain have been shown to upset neurological functioning, and it is thus logical to assume that their constant ingestion will lead to a constant imbalance in autonomic functioning (prolonged stress).

Dr. Ballentine also points out that since World War II the consumption of soft drinks has gone up by eighty percent, pastries by seventy percent and potato chips by eighty-five percent. (On the other hand, the consumption of dairy products has decreased by twenty-one percent, vegetables by twenty-three percent and fruits by twenty-five percent.) Needless to say, the main ingredients found in snack foods are sugar, refined flour, salt and chemical additives that enhance flavor and color—and extend shelf-life. There can be little doubt that this will adversely affect our levels of stress.

Even the nature of the "nutritious" food that we consume has been adversely altered in the past twenty years. "Convenience," or processed, foods have become increasingly popular since World War II, but they are notoriously lacking in both nutritional value and fiber. It is well-known among old country doctors that when the farm family stopped growing and preparing its own food and began to eat "store-bought" food, the incidence of disease increased in that family. This is further supported by the remarkable work of Dr. Weston Price in his research on dietary habits in primitive cultures. Fortunately, as we increase our knowledge of the importance of good dietary habits and organic, "natural" foods, our diets are shifting toward a more wholesome fare in which fresh, whole and unrefined foods are prepared for immediate consumption.

One means of reducing chronic stress is to begin learning about nutrition and to begin paying attention to how the food we eat affects us both mentally and physically. For example, no one need question whether or not refined sugar creates internal stress. Simply pay attention to your body, and it will tell you. Try an experiment. Some morning eat a breakfast consisting of a bottle of soda pop, a piece of chocolate cake and a package of potato chips. Then record how you feel for the next few hours—or days. Wait a few days, and then eat a breakfast consisting of very sweet apples, pears and/or pineapple along with some whole grain bread (without additives). The difference between the natural food and the popular "snack food" will be very apparent to you. No one will ever again be able to tell you that refined sugar and naturally-occurring sugars are the same.

This experiment will not only point out (rather dramatically) the effect of food on the body and mind, it will also point out the body's capacity for determining whether or not the food is good for it. This leads us to the question of how we eat, and the effect this has on our levels of stress.

The Importance of How We Eat

As Swami Rama points out in *A Practical Guide to Holistic Health*, how we eat is just as important as what we eat, but most of us are in too much of a hurry to take the time to really chew and taste our food. After two, three or four quick chews, we swallow it, expecting the poor system to break it down further. But contrary to what seems to be popular belief, the liver does not have teeth. It cannot adequately break down swallow-size pieces.

There are several important consequences of gulping down food. One is that the digestive process is incomplete. The nutritional absorption as well as the proper mixture of food and digestive enzymes (which are supposed to take place in the mouth) are bypassed. Thus, the digestive process is interrupted, and digestion is incomplete. This leads, of course, to stress within the entire system—and when gulping food becomes a consistent habit, we have a significant source of chronic stress.

It is also true that if we gulp down our food we do not taste it. Only a few strong flavors—sweetness, saltiness and sourness—are experienced. The more subtle flavors (which require a more complete breakdown of the food as it mixes with the digestive juices) are not tasted. Thus, we don't allow our taste buds to tell us what is good for us (it tastes good) and what may not be (it tastes bad).

Most processed food, and in particular, snack food (so-called "junk food") is intentionally designed to appeal to the obvious tastes—sweet, salty and/or sour. They contain either sugar and/or salt as a major ingredient, and eating fast will leave this taste in the mouth. Their real appearance, odor and flavor are disguised by a variety of chemicals. The words *enhanced* or *imitation* on the label usually mean that this has happened.

While artificial colorings can fool the eyes, it is much more difficult to fool the nose—and it is even more difficult to fool the taste buds. Our taste habits are primarily conditioned by the few strong flavors, and gulping food simply reinforces the dependency upon them. But if you give your olfactory and taste capacities a chance to do their work, it is very difficult to hide or "enhance" the real flavor or smell of what you are putting into your mouth.

There is an experiment which will give you an opportunity to discover for yourself your potential for tasting food. You will need two pieces of bread. One should be the fluffy white kind made from highly refined enriched white flour, complete with all sorts of artificial additives (chemicals). The other should be a piece of fresh whole grain flour bread made without any additives or preservatives. Rinse your mouth with water. Then take the white fluffy bread, hold it to your nose and sniff several times to get a good smell. Then put it into your mouth and chew until it becomes liquid. Spit it out, rinse your mouth, and repeat the same process with the whole grain flour bread. Does your taste and smell tell you anything about which bread you should be eating?

This same experiment should be tried comparing a piece of snack food (such as a packaged chocolate cupcake) with a piece of fresh fruit. Make sure you chew each until there is nothing but liquid in the mouth. Give your taste buds a chance to work.

Another reason not to gulp food is that when it is chewed completely, we will generally eat about a third less than if we "wolf" it down. Since digestion is taking place more efficiently when we do this, hunger is satisfied more quickly and thoroughly, and this requires less intake. Compulsive eaters, or overeaters, rarely, if ever, really chew their food. So if this is a problem for you, taking the time to chew your food will be very helpful.

Eating when one is calm and quiet is also helpful. The emotional disturbances of anger, sadness and/or fear create an "impossible" internal environment for the digestive process, and even the most perfect food creates serious digestive difficulties when eaten under these conditions. When our ancestors offered up a silent prayer before meals, it gave them a time to clear the mind of disturbing emotions—and thus calm the body—before they ate. Silent prayer cultivated an attitude of thankfulness and prepared the mind and body to receive grace in the form of food. It allowed the mind to focus on positive, joyful emotions, cleansing out whatever destructive feelings were there and calming the body. This, of course, led to parasympathetic dominance and the proper neurological balance required for efficient digestion. Somewhere along the way we modern, knowledgeable people have lost the simple wisdom of our ancestors. Instead of being the center of peace, the dinner table is all too often a battleground. The price we pay for this is reflected in the epidemic of digestive tract diseases that we suffer from today.

Eating in Haste

The third way we create stress by our dietary habits is when we eat. Digestion takes place under the control of the parasympathetic nervous system, so if sympathetic arousal is dominant, then the digestive process is inhibited and stress is inevitable. While this is somewhat oversimplified, it is essentially correct to say that the extent to which we are in a state of arousal (sympathetic dominance) determines the extent of digestion that can take place. So the pervasive habit of "grabbing a bite to eat" or "eating on the run" almost guarantees that one is going to suffer digestive stress. And the more frequently one does this, the more likely it is to lead to constant stress. Yet how many times do we approach our meals with any degree of calm?

Not restricting our intake of food to times that are appropriate to the tasks that we impose on ourselves is another source of stress. Constantly snacking (and thus requiring the body's digestive process to be continually working) is part of this problem. Eating before bedtime, or eating right before or soon after engaging in strenuous mental or physical activity is another part of it. Asking the body to perform two neurologically opposing tasks is to invite stress. For example—wining, dining and then lovemaking is the romantic ideal, but its very real consequence is decreased digestive efficiency, decreased sexual capacity and increased stress. It is far more practical (and far less stressful) to first make love and then wine and dine. This way you are not asking your physiology to perform two conflicting activities at the same time. If performed in proper order, all activities are enhanced—your nervous system, your digestive system and your relationship all benefit.

The following passage from *Diet and Nutrition* by Rudolph Ballentine, M.D., illustrates the importance of proper dietary habits.

When properly trained, appetite, tastes and bodily cues can be a very accurate and dependable source of information about what one needs nutritionally. Moreover, they change from moment to moment and keep one current as to what is needed and what is not. If we are emotionally upset we lose our appetites. This is the way our physiology has of advising us that digestion would be difficult at this time. Unfortunately, these cues are not always acknowledged or recognized. Too often the small, still voice of our inner urgings is overwhelmed by the noise around us—the force of our habits, the pressure of peer groups and the curiosity to try things for which we have no real appetite. Too often we eat according to our schedules and according to what is convenient rather than according to our needs.

There is a story told in the East of two fakirs who had spent years in seclusion studying yoga, learning extraordinary feats of physical and mental control and mastery of their minds and bodies. Standing on the banks of the Ganges, they fell into one another's company, and in the course of their conversation one of them happened to imply that he had developed the ability to do more miraculous things than most, probably including his companion.

The other fakir, a bit older and perhaps a bit wiser, rebuked him gently, wondering whether he might not be carried away by a moment's boastfulness. But his new-found friend bristled with pride and volunteered to demonstrate what he could do.

The older man agreed to this. "Go ahead," he said.

The younger man proceeded, "See the man across the river? I will make appear on a piece of paper in his hand the name of a friend whom he has long forgotten."

The older man smiled, "Is that really the sort of thing you do? That's nothing."

The younger fakir replied, now with some heat, "Oh, really! That's nothing? Well, please tell me, what sort of miraculous feats do *you* accomplish?"

The first fakir looked at him calmly and his eyes twinkled, "I eat when I'm hungry and drink when I'm thirsty."

If one can eat only when hungry and yet, at the same time take his meals with reasonable regularity and at proper intervals, he will have met one of the greatest challenges of good nutrition.

Your dietary habits provide the basis for your physical foundation—your body. By paying attention to what you eat, how you eat and when you eat, as well as the effects these have on you, chronic stress can be significantly reduced.

The Role of Exercise in Stress

In recent years modern man has become very exercise conscious. Tennis, golf, swimming, skiing and the ever-present jogging have become almost institutionalized. Large cities and small towns sponsor marathons (long-distance running competitions—as long as twenty-six miles), in which success is defined as much by completing the course as by winning. Literally thousands of people who have no hope of winning, train and jog their sneakers off just in order to qualify to run in a major marathon. Corporations of all sizes are installing gyms, handball courts and tennis courts in order to encourage their employees to participate in some form of exercise.

Increased health, happiness and productivity are the payoffs. Those who exercise consistently are healthier, have less coronary-vascular disease, fewer frustrations, and generally report greater satisfaction with their lives than those who do not. They also have fewer medical expenses and ingest smaller quantities of drugs.

Much has been written about exercise and no one seriously disputes the fact that it is necessary to maintain a healthy body and mind. Nearly everything that has been said or written about physical fitness, however, focuses upon one area—that of strengthening or increasing the vital capacity of the various internal organ systems or the musculature. The focus is on the physical involvement, with little emphasis on the mental. Although there is increasing recognition that physical fitness "invigorates the brain," and that sports offer an opportunity to get your mind off work, the primary focus is on muscular strength and endurance, cardiovascular endurance, flexibility and physical balance.

While it is true that recent work at the University of Wisconsin at Madison has begun to explore the relationship between jogging and depression, this is the exception and not the rule in exercise literature. Most people exercise only for their bodies, unaware that exercise is also an excellent way to understand the mind for the specific purpose of altering non-helpful mental states and emotional habits.

If one were to examine his own physical fitness experience, however, he would soon recognize that there were times when his sport was unsatisfying. This was not the fault of the exercise, nor is it helpful to blame it on an "off" day. What was wrong is that the mind was not as involved as it could have been. And whenever the body is exercising and the mind is not involved with it, the exercise itself will yield fewer benefits. In fact, if one is merely pushing the body but paying no attention to it at all, exercise can be harmful.

A classic example of this is the Type A personality who has been told by his doctor to start jogging every day. So, in true type A form, he compulsively sets up a schedule of jogging in which he attempts to achieve certain goals as quickly as possible. After all, if he is going to run, then by God he will be the best runner in the block. He runs against the clock just as he works against the clock, and the result is that he has added another strain to his day rather than a beneficial play for his body. Working or jogging, it is his mental attitude that is creating his stress. The activity follows the mental event.

This point is very important to understand: *For exercise to be effective in significantly altering chronic levels of stress, the attentional faculty of the mind must be on the activity itself and not wandering into past and future imagery.* Mind and body and action must be coordinated. For establishing this coordination the mind must be trained to pay attention—and attention is the key to success. When this takes place, there will be no residue of stress even though there may be strong physiological arousal that requires a consequent period of relaxation.

Remember that stress is the consequence of extraneous demands for action being programmed into the body by mental preoccupation with emotionally loaded future or past events. That is, when mind/body/action are not coordinated the result is stress. This also explains why competitive sports may be very stress-producing, particularly when there are heavy emotional attachments (such as financial or self-esteem considerations), involved with winning or losing.

The power of concentration (maintaining a one-pointed mind) and the ability of the mind to increase performance skills is becoming increasingly recognized by both professional and amateur athletes. In such books as Timothy Galway's *The Inner Game of Tennis*, for instance, the use of concentration and mental imagery (actually performing the actions perfectly in the mind before performing the actions with the body) has proven to be of great help in developing skills and performance, for whatever the mind has decided, the body does. However, the focus is still on the performance; it is still at the level of the external body.

The use of exercise to increase conscious awareness of internal physiological events as well as to calm the mind, is seldom, if ever, recognized in Western physical fitness programs where there is an attempt to perfect strength and physical coordination. In the East, on the other hand, the attempt is to perfect control of the mind over the body. We should not try to become Easterners, but we can adopt those programs which will increase our conscious control over mental/emotional events and mind/body interactions—and thus bring balance to our physical fitness regimens.

Exercise for Mind/Body Coordination

The relationship between mind and body is very complex, for they are interrelated and interdependent. While it is true that the mind has the ultimate control, it is equally true that events in the body will deeply affect the mind. If you have doubts about this, simply spend a few hours all hunched over and see how you feel. Some of the most common symptoms of chronic stress are stiff muscles, backaches and painful joints. Stress is retained in the body through muscle tension, and this problem is exacerbated when the tendons become short and rigid, allowing for little flexibility and leading to sprains, torn ligaments and muscles and dislocated joints. More serious, and also stress-related, is arthritis, the crippling joint disease.

We inherently recognize stored tension when we realize that we must loosen up the back muscles before playing handball or tennis, and exercises which systematically stretch muscles and tendons are very important. So what do we do to warm up? A few jumping jacks, shrug the shoulders, a few quick deep-knee bends, running in place, or some other quick, short and choppy movement. All to get our muscles ready to go! Unfortunately, this is the wrong way to stretch muscles!

To relieve tension, to stretch and loosen tight muscles and tendons, requires slow, sustained movement together with holding the stretched posture. Pumping muscles with quick movements does not stretch them out; it builds more tension within them. It will probably energize the muscle, it is true, but it will not release tension.

There are a wide variety of simple stretching exercises available (at the end of this chapter are several which are excellent for stress reduction). But there is a secret to doing stretches that is very important—coordinate your breathing with the movement. This will improve your capacity dramatically. In other words, if you pay close attention to both the movement and the breath, you will be able to determine whether that movement should be done on an exhalation or an inhalation. A general rule is that whenever the body is stretched back, you should inhale. Whenever the body, or any part of it is stretched down, or bent over, you should exhale during the movement. When you coordinate the movement with the breath, you are coordinating the mind with the movement, for the breath reflects the various conditions of the mind. Breath coordination will also insure that the movements will not be too fast.

Breath is also an important variable in the other half of stretching exercises—holding the stretch. For example, when you stretch down to touch your toes, you should not bob up and down as if you were bobbing for apples in a tub of water. (Even if this does not pull a muscle, your stretching in this fashion will be of little benefit.) Rather, bend down to touch your toes, and then stay bent as far as you comfortably can. Do not bend until you feel pain. You are exercising, not taking a course in pain control!

Do not hold your breath. That will only increase tension! After a few moments, concentrate on relaxing the point in the body at which you feel the stretch most. Then, on an exhalation, bend a little bit more, and hold the stretch. Concentrating on the flow of the breath, relax into this posture as much as possible. Then, after a few moments, raise up slowly and relax standing up. The longer you are able to comfortably hold the stretch, the more benefit you will achieve from it. Slowly increase your capacity to hold or remain in the stretch posture. Work within your capacity— and your capacity will certainly increase. Go beyond your capacity—and you will certainly suffer.

With concentration and comfortable breathing, you will be able to stretch much further than you thought. However, utilize the exhalation and bending technique only once or twice after the initial bend. Otherwise you may extend yourself too far, and you will feel that overextension for the next few days.

By moving gently and relaxing into the posture (holding the limit of the stretch) one can begin to develop the most necessary skill that comes from exercising. That is, *by paying close attention to the internal feelings, movements and patterns while doing the exercise or movement, you can develop conscious sensitivity to the subtle feedback cues of that physiological process. This developing sensitivity leads to a greater conscious control over that physiological process.*

In other words, you are learning how to use your own innate biofeedback machine. This is exactly what must be done if exercise is to lead to mastery over chronic stress. Without developing this internal awareness, you will never develop control over chronic tension in the body and its various systems, particularly in the musculature.

For example, as we mentioned earlier, most people are not sensitive to the tension level in the shoulders and neck until there is stiffness, soreness and pain—or even a headache. The pain is finally needed in order to grab your attention. The problem lies not in the shoulders. These muscles are only following instructions, and all along they have been signaling back to the brain with every tiny change or increase in tension. The problem is that no one was at home up in the brain. No one was paying attention to the feedback signals. Consequently, the muscle had to continue to maintain its levels of tension.

It is not only possible, but necessary, to develop your sensitivity so that the muscles are never allowed to acquire such extensive and chronic levels of tension—and this can be done by concentrating on the muscles during stretching exercises and during relaxation. If you do the stretches and are thinking about how wonderful you look doing them, or how far you can bend in comparison to others, or about your job, or about anything else, you have largely wasted your time. You will not have been aware of the most important elements of the exercise—the changing internal physical and mental states.

Five minutes of intense concentration on a consistent basis will slowly develop your internal awareness. This can be done with all the muscles—the heartbeat, blood pressure, and just about any system in the body—but, most of us would not want to spend the amount of time necessary to control our heartbeat to any great degree. Very little time, however, is needed to develop sensitivity to, and control over, the muscles—which are the primary targets of stress.

Body, Mind and Consciousness

Hatha yoga is a practical exercise system designed to work with and through the body in order to expand conscious awareness of both mind and body. The purpose is to lead one systematically from physical exercises, to breathing exercises to mental exercises—and to achieve a higher level of awareness.

On the physical level the hatha yoga system strengthens various organ, glandular and neurological systems. In addition, it reduces physical tension by slowly stretching the muscles and tendons and by eliminating those habitual patterns in the physical being which sustain stress. It consists of stretches and held postures, alternated with relaxation, which allow the mind and body to be fully coordinated; it also includes the practices which cleanse the body of accumulated toxins and waste products. But the ultimate goal of the system is to bring perfect balance and harmony into the body-mind/spirit relationship and eliminate "dis-ease" conditions.

In the West, the system of hatha yoga has been taught primarily as a beauty cult to keep oneself young and healthy. While this does happen, the real purpose is to calm the mind, increase concentration skills and expand internal awareness. It is not by accident that the postures are centered around the spine and central nervous system. Through proper manipulation, exercise and concentration, the postures directly benefit the particular glandular, structural and organic systems that are involved in that posture.

It is the combination of controlled breathing, physical effects and concentration which leads one to increased awareness. In this way the physiological systems are gradually brought into complete harmony, and this inner balance allows one to sustain deep concentration and a one-pointed mind. This leads to mental equilibrium. These benefits are not achieved by any Western system of exercise.

The system of hatha yoga should be learned from a competent teacher. Beginning exercises, such as the joints and glands exercises and some of the stretches, can, and should be, practiced on your own, and several of the more immediately helpful ones are described at the end of this chapter. The ideal, however, is to find a competent instructor and learn the postures. Then develop a routine that fits your nature and needs.

When selecting a teacher, remember that the ultimate purpose of the system is to work with the mind and internal concentration skills. Therefore, find a teacher who has been trained in this discipline and can effectively teach it. The competent teacher is one who knows his subject well and practices what he teaches. Knowledge of the role of the breath is also vitally important, for it is a necessary part of hatha yoga.

Hatha yoga need not replace sports or aerobic exercises. As Swami Rama pointed out in *A Practical Guide to Holistic Health*, you need balance in your exercise program just as you need balance in the other areas of your life. A short daily period of hatha yoga postures can (and should) supplement your regular routine. The benefits will soon be apparent to you. There is no question but that we need to exercise. We are literally killing ourselves by inactivity (as well as wasting our fullest potential) when even a short daily period of exercise can prevent many physical and mental problems.

Stress Exercises

Below are a series of exercises which anyone can do easily and quickly. They are divided into two sections. The first consists of desk exercises which are taken from *Joints and Glands Exercises* (see bibliography). This little book presents an entire series of simple stretching exercises for the face, neck and shoulders which are designed to increase circulation and decrease tension in the various muscle, joint and glandular areas of the body. They can easily be done while sitting at a desk (and at any time during the day). If practiced often, they will provide immediate benefits in terms of effective stress reduction.

The second set of exercises, relaxation and stretches, are a bit more involved and require some space in which to perform them. They are taken from *Hatha Yoga Manual I* by Samskrti and Veda (see bibliography) which gives one an excellent introduction to hatha yoga postures followed by a relaxation as well as a series of beginning stretching exercises. The book is authoritative and provides clear step-by-step instructions which are illustrated. Stretching exercises are necessary to eliminate tension in the body as well as to loosen muscles and lengthen tendons, and the manual outlines nine points that should be followed when doing them:

1. Set a specific time each day for your practice—this should be when you are not rushed. Practice at least a little every day.

2. Morning and evening are the two best times to practice. Morning exercise helps you remain calm and alert during the day. In the evening, the exercises help relieve the day's tensions so that you can enjoy a peaceful night's sleep.

3. Do the exercises in a clean, quiet and well-ventilated room. Wear loose, comfortable clothing.

4. Always practice on an empty stomach.

5. Women should not practice strenuous exercises during menstruation.

6. Do not become discouraged if your body does not respond the same way each day. Just keep practicing regularly, and don't compete with others.

7. Study your body and its movements. Be aware of your capacity and learn not to go beyond it. Your capacity will increase with practice.

8. Let the body movements flow evenly and gently with the breath. Do not hold your breath at any time.

9. Follow any exertion with relaxation. However, do not allow the mind to drift toward sleep while you relax.

Remember, the purpose of the stretches is to relieve tension and to increase your internal awareness and control of bodily processes. Concentrate on what you are doing. Keep the breath even, steady and coordinated with the movement. Enjoy the exercises.

Desk Exercises

Forehead and Sinus Massage
1. Sit in a comfortable posture with the head, neck and trunk straight. Make a loose fist with both hands, the thumbs against the forehead between the two eyebrows. Begin to massage the forehead with the thumbs by working up and out with a stroking motion. Follow the bony structure

around the eyes and continue out across the temples.

2. Next, place the side of the thumbs on the face just below the eyes and next to the nose, one on each side. Make the same motions, moving outwards across the face and temples.

3. Open the hands. Using the undersides of the thumbs, gently slide the thumbs across the upper rim of the eye sockets towards the temples.

4. Likewise, massage with the index fingers the lower rim of the eye sockets towards the temples.

All of these movements begin at the center of the face and move outward. This pushes all the tension off the face, forehead and temples and smoothes away any wrinkles on the forehead or crows-feet at the eye edges. This massage may help break up and loosen mucus obstructions in the nasal sinuses.

Eyes

Keep the head stationary and facial muscles relaxed in the following eye exercises. For several seconds after each variation, relax the eyes by gently closing them. All eye exercises can be done three times in each direction.

1. Start with the eyes straight forward, then slowly turn them to the left as far as comfortable. Feel the stretch in the eye muscles, slowly come back to the forward position.

Look to the right in the same manner, and again return to the forward position. Always balance what you do on one side by doing the same thing on the opposite side, holding the stretch for the same length of time in each direction.

2. Turn the eyes towards the ceiling, then bring the eyes back to the forward position. Look down, and again

bring the eyes back to the forward position.

3.   Look to the upper left-hand corner of your eye socket. Bring the eyes back to the forward position. Look to the lower right-hand corner and return the eyes to the forward position.

4.   Look at the lower left-hand corner; return to the forward position. Look towards the upper right-hand corner and again back to the forward position. Relax by closing the eyes.

5.   First look downward; then start the eyes rolling in a clockwise motion, making a complete circle. Reverse the process, moving the eyes in a counter-clockwise direction. The movements should be slow and free from jerks. Relax by closing the eyes.

6.   Close the eyes and squeeze the lids together very tightly for five seconds. Now blink the eyelids as rapidly as you can. Relax by closing the eyes gently so that the eyelids barely touch.

You can give the eyes a warmth-bath by rubbing the palms of the hands quickly together until the hands become very hot. Then gently lay the palms of the hands on the closed eyelids, allowing the heat from the skin to permeate the eyelids.

Neck

These exercises are very good for relieving accumulated tension in the back neck muscles. If you have tension head-aches or are bothered by a stiff neck and shoulders, these will be very helpful, and can be practiced several times daily without any difficulty.

1.   *Forward and Backward Bend:* Exhale slowly,

bringing the head forward and taking the chin towards the chest. Feel the stretch of the muscles in the back of the neck. Inhale slowly, lifting the head up and back, stretching the muscles of the front of the neck. With an exhalation, slowly return to the forward position.

2. *Chin over Shoulder:* With an exhalation, turn the head as far to the left as possible and try to bring the chin in line with the shoulder. Inhale and bring the head back to the forward position. Repeat in the same manner on the right side.

3. *Ear over Shoulder:* With an exhalation, bring the left ear towards the left shoulder. Inhale and come back to the center. Exhale and bring the right ear towards the right shoulder. Again inhale, come back to the center and relax. Only the head and neck should move. The shoulder should not be raised to meet the ear.

4. *Turtle:* Keeping the shoulders stationary, exhale and thrust the chin and head as far forward as comfortable, keeping the mouth closed and the teeth together. Inhaling, slowly come back to the center; then moving the head back, tuck the chin into the neck, forcing an extreme double chin. Exhale and relax, returning to the center position.

5. *Neck Rolls:* Lower the chin to the chest and slowly begin to rotate the head in a clockwise direction. Inhale while lifting the head up and back and exhale when bringing it forward and down. Reverse and rotate the same number of times in the opposite, counter-clockwise direction. The head, neck and body should be relaxed, allowing the head to rotate freely and loosely.

6. *Lion Posture:* While sitting in a chair, lean forward. Throw the shoulders forward, exhale and thrust the chin and

head as far forward as comfortable, opening the mouth wide and thrusting the tongue out and down, trying to touch the chin. At the same time, place hands on the knees, arms straight, with fingers widely spread, exerting a pull on hands, arms and shoulders. The eyes should be focused on the point between the two eyebrows. The whole body should be stretched. Hold the breath while briefly holding this position. Sit back and relax with an inhalation, and repeat.

Shoulders

Stand or sit with the arms hanging loosely at the sides. Begin to rotate the left shoulder in a complete circle, first moving it forward and in towards the center of the chest, exhaling as you do. Then move it up towards the ear and back while inhaling, trying to touch the shoulder-blade to the spine, and then down back into the starting position. Rotate three times in this direction and then reverse and rotate three times in the opposite direction. Do the same for the right shoulder, and then do both shoulders together. Relax.

These simple exercises can easily be done several times during the day (be sure to coordinate the breathing with the movement). They not only stretch the muscles but also increase one's sensitivity to the inner movements and feelings associated with them. This, in turn, will evolve into increased control and reduce the chronic tension in the muscles.

Relaxation

The Corpse Posture

Lie on the back and gently close the eyes. Place the feet a comfortable distance apart; place the arms along the sides of the body, with the palms upward and the fingers gently curled. The legs should not touch each other, nor should the arms and hands touch the body. Do not lie haphazardly or place the limbs far apart, but lie in a symmetrical position. Breathe diaphragmatically with even, steady breaths. Concentrate on eliminating all pauses, jerks and shakiness in the breath, making the breath as smooth as possible.

In this posture the body resembles a corpse in the sense that it lies still and relaxed. It is important to refrain from drowsing; keep the mind alert and focused on the flow of the breath.

Between stretches, remain in this position only until respiration and heartbeat return to normal. While relaxing before and after the sequence of stretches, beginners should not remain in this position for more than ten minutes.

Before doing the stretches to follow, this posture centers the mind and prepares it for focusing on the body. It helps you to relax the skeletal muscles, enabling you to go further into the stretches while reducing the likelihood of injuries. Between stretches, it helps you to relax and to prepare the mind for the next exercise in sequence. After the exercises it reduces all traces of fatigue. At midday, as a break from your work, it relaxes and rejuvenates the mind and body.

Stretches

Side Stretch

Assume a simple standing posture. Begin inhaling, and slowly raise the right arm out to the side with the palm facing downward. When the arm reaches shoulder level, turn the palm upward. Continue inhaling and raise the arm until it is next to the ear. Still continuing to inhale and keeping the feet firmly on the floor, stretch the entire right side of the body upward. Then, without allowing the body to bend forward or backward or the right arm to bend, begin exhaling and slowly bend at the waist, sliding the left hand down the left leg. Breathe evenly for three complete breaths. Inhaling, slowly bring the body back to an upright position. Exhaling, slowly lower the arm to shoulder level, turn the palm downward, and return to the simple standing posture. Concentrate on the breath until the body relaxes completely. Repeat the side stretch in the opposite direction.

Note: For a more intense stretch repeat this posture with the legs together.

Simple Back Stretch

Assume the standing posture.

With the fingers facing downward, place the heels of the hands on either side of the spine just above the buttocks. Exhaling, gently push the hips forward, slowly letting the head, neck and trunk bend backward as far as comfortable without straining. Inhaling, return to the standing pose, keeping the hands in the same position. Keeping the entire body relaxed, slowly bend the body forward as far as possible. Hold this position until all the muscles of the back relax completely.

Note: This forward bend balances the effects of the backward bend.

Angle Posture

Assume the simple standing posture with the feet two to three feet apart. Placing the arms behind the back, grasp the right wrist with the left hand. Keep the heels in line and place the right foot at a 90° angle from the left. (Beginning students may turn the left foot slightly inward—to the right—if it is more comfortable.) Inhaling, turn the body toward the right foot. Exhaling, bend forward from the hips and bring the head as close to the knee as comfortable. Breathe evenly; hold this position for five counts. Inhaling, slowly raise the body, exhaling, turn to the front. Turn the right foot so that it faces forward. Repeat the exercise on the left side.

Second Position: Keeping the arms straight, interlace the fingers behind the back. With the right foot at a 90° angle from the left, turn the body and bend forward from the hips, bringing the head toward the right knee. Raise the hands overhead as far as comfortable. Breathe evenly; hold this position for five counts. Inhaling, slowly raise the body and turn to the front. Repeat the exercise on the left side. Repeat the exercise to the front, with both feet facing forward.

Third Position: With the arms straight, interlace the fingers behind the back and press the palms together. Exhaling, raise the arms and bend forward as far as comfortable. Breathe evenly and hold for five counts. Inhaling, push the hands toward the floor and bend the head, neck and trunk back as far as comfortable without straining. Breathe evenly; hold for five counts. Slowly return to a standing position and relax.

Torso Twist

Assume the simple standing posture with the feet two to three feet apart. Raise the arms overhead; interlace the fingers. Keeping the arms next to the ears and stretching the body from the rib cage upward, rotate the upper torso, arms, and hands in a clockwise direction. The waist, hips and legs remain stationary. Inhale as the body leans to the right and to the back; exhale as the body leans to the left and to the front. Repeat three times clockwise and then three times counterclockwise. Continue by moving into the second position.

Second Position: Keeping the hips stationary and bending from the waist, repeat the above exercise three times clockwise and three times counterclockwise. Continue by moving into the third position. (Remember to breathe as described in the first position.)

Third Position: Keeping the legs stationary and bending from the hips as far as comfortable, rotate and twist the entire upper part of the body in a large circle. Repeat three times clockwise and three times counterclockwise. (Remember to breathe as described in the first position.)

Relax. Concentrate on the breath.

Complete your exercise period by lying on your back, breathing diaphragmatically and concentrating on the breath for five minutes. This is an excellent time to practice 2:1 Breathing as described at the end of Chapter 7.

Sun Salutation

This is an integrated exercise that stretches and limbers the spine as well as all of the limbs and joints. The sun salutation is a series of twelve positions, each flowing into the next in one graceful, continuous movement. First become familiar with the movements, and then coordinate the breath with them. You will find, as you progress from doing two or three every morning to doing seven or eight or more, that you will feel the difference on the days you do not do them. (This is the author's favorite wake-up exercise.) The benefits are innumerable. The following directions are taken from *Hatha Yoga Manual I:*

"While asleep, the body lies in an inactive condition. During this time, the conscious mind ceases to function, the metabolic rate decreases, circulation of the body fluids slows and the functional capacity of the rest of the body is considerably reduced. Upon awakening, the body and mind must make a transition from this inactive condition to one of activity. The sun salutation aids in this transition by massaging and stimulating the glands, organs, muscles and nerves of the body. The breath rate increases, bringing more oxygen into the lungs, thus quickening the heart rate. This in turn causes more blood to pass through the lungs, picking up oxygen, and therefore sending a greater supply of oxygenated blood throughout the different parts of the body."

In other words, doing the sun salutation energizes the body. It's a wonderful exercise. Try it for a month, gradually increasing the number of salutations you do each morning until you are doing at least eight to twelve. You will notice the difference in how you feel for the rest of the day.

Position One: (Exhaling during movement) Stand firmly with the head, neck and trunk in a straight line. Beginners can stand with the feet slightly apart. With palms together in prayer position, place the hands before the heart and gently close the eyes. Standing silently, concentrate on the breath.

Position Two: (Inhaling during movement) Inhaling, slightly lower and stretch the hands and arms forward with the palms facing downward. Raise the arms overhead until they are next to the ears. Keeping the legs straight and the head between the arms, arch the spine and bend backward as far as possible without straining.

Position Three: (Exhaling during movement) Exhaling, bend forward from the hips, keeping the back straight and the arms next to the ears. Continue bending; place the palms next to the feet, aligning the fingers with the toes. Bring

the head to the knees keeping the legs straight. Note: If you cannot place the hands on the floor without beinding the legs, then lower only as far as comfortable without straining.

Position Four: (Inhaling during movement)   In this position bend the knees if necessary in order to place the hands on the floor. Inhaling, stretch the right leg back, rest the right knee and the top of the right foot on the floor, and extend the toes. The left foot remains between the hands; the hands remain firmly on the floor. Arch the back, look up, and stretch the head back as far as comfortable. The line from the head to the tip of the right foot should form a smooth and graceful curve.

Position Five: (Retain the breath)   Retain the breath. (This is the only position in which the breath is held.) Curl the toes of the right foot, extend the left leg, placing it next to the right.

The arms remain straight and the body forms an inclined plane from the head to the feet. This position resembles a starting push-up position.

Position Six: (Exhale during movement) Exhaling, drop first the knees, and then the chest to the floor, keeping the tips of the fingers in line with the breasts. Tuck in the chin and place the forehead on the floor. In this position only the toes, knees, hands, chest, and forehead touch the floor. The nose does not touch the floor and the elbows remain close to the body.

Position Seven: (Inhale during movement) Without moving the hands and forehead, relax the legs and extend the feet so that the body rests flat on the floor. Inhaling, slowly raise the head. First, touch the nose and then chin to the floor; then stretch the head forward and upward. Without using the strength of the arms or hands, slowly raise

the shoulders and chest; look up and bend back as far as comfortable. In this posture the navel remains on the floor. To lift the thorax, use the muscles of the back only. Do not use the arms and hands to push the body off the floor, but to balance the body. Keep the feet and legs together and relaxed.

Position Eight: (Exhale during movement) Without repositioning the feet and hands, straighten the feet so that they point towards the hands. Exhaling, straighten the arms and push the buttocks high in the air. Bring the head between the arms and try to gently press the heels to the floor.

Position Nine: (Inhaling during movement) Inhaling, bend the right knee and place the right foot between the hands. Align the toes with the fingers. Rest the left knee and the top of the foot on the floor and extend the toes. Arch the back, look up, and

bend back as far as comfortable.

Position   Ten: (Exhaling
during movement)   Exhaling,
place the left foot beside the
right keeping the palms on the
floor. Straighten the legs and
bring the head to the knees.

Position   Eleven: (Inhaling
during movement)   Inhaling,
slowly raise the body, stretching the arms out, up and back.
Remember to keep the arms
next to the ears and to keep
the legs straight.

Position Twelve: (Exhaling)
Exhaling, return to an erect
standing position. Slowly lower the arms and bring the
hands to the chest in prayer
position. Repeat the sun salutation, but alternate the leg
movements by extending the
opposite leg in positions four
and nine. Then relax as described.

The Breath of Life

Because of its unique relationship to the autonomic nervous system, the breath plays a vital role in determining whether or not we suffer from stress. To begin with, our breath functions either voluntarily or involuntarily. That is, we can either regulate our breathing consciously or we can forget about it and still continue to breathe without being aware of it. It is this ability (as well as its implications in the relationship of mind/body interaction) which makes the breath so important in the control and elimination of stress.

The relationship between mind and body has always fascinated Western medical science, philosophy and psychology, yet nowhere in the literature is it clearly defined and explicated. In other words, the mind/body relationship is known, but it is not understood. In yoga science, however, this relationship has been systematically researched and defined for literally thousands of years. Through intensive inner concentration, experimentation and study, advanced yogis have explored this complex area and have recognized and verified that the breath is the key mediating factor between mind and body.

The Western sciences, on the other hand, have studied breathing primarily from the perspective of ventilation perfusion and blood gases. While this is one of its central functions, there is another which has just recently begun to be examined—the relationship between breathing and the autonomic and central nervous systems. As it is, we know that changes in neurological functioning are reflected in changes in the breathing pattern. For instance, the emotional state of depression is reflected in the breath by frequent sighing as well as shallow and arrhythmic breathing, while sudden, sharp pain is invariably accompanied by a sharp intake of breath, or gasp. These are just two of the more obvious examples of breathing patterns which reflect mental and physical events.

The breath can also affect (influence, modify) those same mental and physical processes. If you are angry, for instance, you can begin to calm yourself by simply slowing down the flow of the breath and making sure that you don't hold it at any time. It is this causal influence on the nervous system that is so important in controlling and eliminating stress.

Because we in the West have generally overlooked the breath (except when there is a severe pathological condition in the lungs, such as asthma or emphysema), we usually allow it to follow whatever habit pattern has been formed. Unfortunately, this can not only create and maintain a state of constant stress, it can also prevent us from achieving lasting relief from it—no matter how many stretching and relaxation exercises we may practice.

Since breathing is central to both controlling stress and developing concentration, it is important that we understand the physiology of the breathing process—and there are several key points that need to be understood. The first deals with the basic function of the breath: to provide oxygen to the bloodstream which, in turn, takes it to the entire cellular structure. We must also understand the relationship between how we breathe, the autonomic nervous system, and our emotional states. We also need to understand the proper method of breathing as it affects the motion of the lungs, and in turn our health. For example, when shocking news is given to someone, his mind loses its equilibrium. This disturbs the motion of the lungs, and this makes the heartbeat irregular. The irregular heartbeat disrupts the blood flow to the brain, and this further affects the autonomic nervous system and leads to imbalance. Finally, we must understand the importance of breathing through the nose rather than the mouth. All of these processes are interrelated, each affecting the other.

The Physiology of Breath and Its Therapeutic Value

The primary function of the lungs is to provide the mechanism by which oxygen is taken into the lungs and carbon dioxide is removed from the blood. The act of breathing (respiration) brings air into the lungs. This consists, roughly, of 21% oxygen, 78% nitrogen, .9% argon and other gases including carbon dioxide. As the air is brought in, it is dispersed in the tracheal-bronchial "tree" to the smallest functional part of the lung—a small air pocket called an

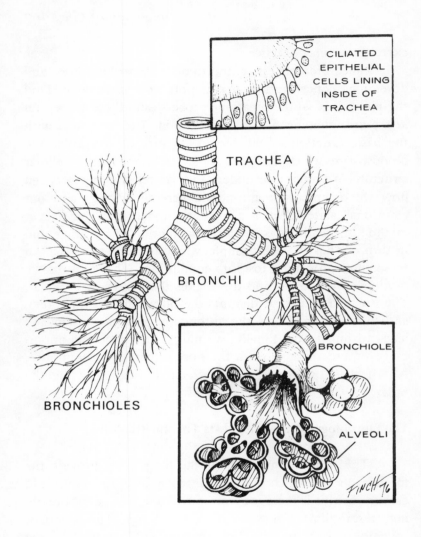

CILIATED
EPITHELIAL
CELLS LINING
INSIDE OF
TRACHEA

TRACHEA

BRONCHI

BRONCHIOLES

BRONCHIOLE

ALVEOLI

Figure 1
THE BRONCHIAL TREE

alveolus which is surrounded by microscopic blood vessels as shown in Figure 1. The lung is shaped, literally, like a tree. The windpipe (trachea) is the main trunk which divides many times into smaller and smaller branches; the alveolus corresponds to the leaf. Just as a tree breathes from its leaves, so do we breathe at the alveoli in the sense that here oxygen diffuses into the blood and carbon dioxide diffuses into the alveolus. Body nutrients, which provide energy fuel to the body, need to burn oxygen (oxidation). This produces carbon dioxide and water, as waste products, which are eliminated from the body through the lungs and kidneys, respectively.

To have a clearer understanding of respiration, imagine the torso as a somewhat flattened cylinder divided into an upper chamber (the chest cavity), and a lower chamber (the abdominal cavity). The chest cavity is defined structurally by the rib cage which provides rigidity. The widest part of the chest cylinder is the lower portion, the area where the ribs have their greatest length of curvature, and most of the space in this cylinder is filled by the lungs.

Inhalation takes place when the cylinder is expanded; the resulting suction pulls air into the lungs. Exhalation takes place when counterpressures (primarily from the elasticity of the lung but also from the external, rigid structure of the chest cavity) force the entire structure back to its original position.

Two major mechanisms provide for the necessary expansion and contraction of the lungs. One is the thoracic mechanism, so-called because the thorax (chest) is expanded and contracted by the intercostal muscles (the specialized muscles which surround and are sandwiched between the ribs). During inhalation the external intercostal muscles pivot the ribs upward and forward, increasing the diameter of the chest and thus pulling air into the lungs. The internal intercostals then perform the opposite function for the exhalation —pulling the ribs downward and thus reducing lung volume. This is thoracic (or chest) breathing, and unfortunately it is the habitual breathing pattern for most of the population. We say "unfortunately," because it is this pattern which is intimately involved with stress.

The other major mechanism for breathing is the diaphragm which can also bring air into the thoracic cavity. As shown in Figure 2, this is a large, dome-shaped sheet of muscle which forms the floor of the chest cavity, separating

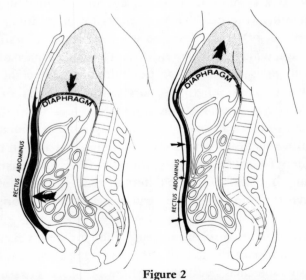

Figure 2
SYNERGISTIC EFFECT OF RECTUS ABDOMINUS MUSCLE
AND DIAPHRAGM ON FORCED EXPIRATION

it from the abdominal cavity. When it contracts, it is pulled taut, or flattened, creating a vacuum, and air is thus pulled into the lungs. When one is standing or sitting, exhalation takes place when the abdominal muscles (acting as the "antagonist" muscles to the diaphragm) contract slightly, pushing the organs back and up. This forces the relaxed diaphragm into its original dome-shaped position and reduces chest cavity volume. It is a significant part of exhalation. When one is lying down gravity serves as the "antagonist" to the diaphragm, pulling the raised belly down and forcing the flexible abdominal organs up. This also pushes the diaphragm back into its dome-shaped original position, and it is part of exhalation. Exhalation takes place primarily because of the elasticity of the lungs, through their ability to recoil through surface tension. Depending on which breathing mechanism is used, the intercostal and abdominal muscles can and do augment exhalation, countering the force of gravity.

Diaphragmatic breathing gently massages the internal organs, pushing them back and forth. This is thought to contribute to proper blood perfusion in these organs and to be one of the driving forces behind the normal peristalsis of the intestines. The massaging does not take place during thoracic breathing. Diaphragmatic breathing is also a very important tool in controlling stress. To understand its full importance, we need to examine the contributions it makes to healthy and relaxed functioning. These are:

Increased efficiency of the cardio-pulmonary system.

Maintaining a non-aroused, relaxed state, countering

physiological arousal which occurs during thoracic (chest) breathing.

Regulation of the respiratory movement (the actual flow of breath) in and out of the body.

Cardio-Pulmonary Efficiency—Taking the Work Out of Breathing

Blood is pumped from the heart directly to the tiny air sacs called alveoli, and there fresh oxygen molecules are exchanged in the bloodstream for carbon dioxide molecules (which are returned as waste products from the cells via the veinous system). Then the blood, being freshly osygenated (energized), returns directly to the heart and is pumped to the entire body. This gas exchange is absolutely essential if cells are to continue to live, for without freshly oxygenated blood the cells of all the tissues will cease functioning. Strokes, for example, take place when the blood flow to the brain is interrupted—certain areas of the brain begin to die. Depending on which cells are affected, and how many cells, one either dies, becomes paralyzed, loses the ability to hear, see or speak, or suffers from a variety of other symptoms.

The first of the freshly oxygenated blood goes directly to the heart itself, keeping that muscle supplied with life-giving oxygen. Most heart attacks (called infarctions) are the result of insufficient oxygen-rich blood getting to the heart, generally because of clogged arteries (or arteriosclerosis). This results in the death of heart muscle cells. There may be warning signs such as severe chest pain (angina pectoris), and this is a signal that the heart is being starved of oxygen and that the cells are beginning to die. If this continues, it interferes with the electrical activity of the heart—and thus with its pumping action.

How does diaphragmatic breathing relate to this? Doesn't thoracic, or chest, breathing supply oxygen to the blood? Yes it does, but not efficiently.

Figure 3 shows the distribution of blood in the lungs. Because of gravity, most of the blood distribution for gas exchange takes place in the lower half of the lungs. When we breathe with the chest wall, the expansion of that wall pulls air into the top two-thirds of the lungs, as shown in Figure 4. Consequently, the gas exchange is inefficient, making the heart and lungs work harder to accomplish the proper amount of oxygenation.

On the other hand, in diaphragmatic breathing the air is pulled all the way down into the blood-rich lower lobes illustrated in Figure 5. This increases the efficiency of the entire cardio-respiratory functioning.

Whichever way one breathes, there is no difference in the amount of oxygen consumed by the body, but there is a vast difference in the amount of work required by the lungs and heart to accomplish the same amount of oxygenation. In fact, the workload of the cardio-respiratory system may be reduced by as much as fifty percent by changing from thoracic to diaphragmatic breathing. This can be seen in the number of times one breathes per minute. While those who chronically breathe with the thoracic mechanism will average about sixteen to twenty breaths per minute, those who breathe habitually with the diaphragm average only six to eight breaths per minute. In one twenty-four hour period, for instance, chronic chest breathers will take 22,000 to 25,000 breaths, while habitual diaphragmatic breathers will take only 10,000 to 12,000. This is a significant difference.

Many of us confuse the terms, *habitual breathing* and *natural breathing.* Most of us believe that our own breathing pattern is natural for us, when the truth is that it is shaped primarily by habit. Natural breathing can best be seen in a healthy infant. If you observe one closely, you will see little or no movement of the chest when it breathes—only the stomach goes up and down (which indicates diaphragmatic breathing). But when the infant is under stress (through hunger or discomfort) and begins to cry, you will see the chest moving in and out in rhythm with the diaphragm.

As we grow up, however, we develop poor and unhealthy breathing habits which replace the natural breathing patterns we are born with, and eventually we no longer utilize the diaphragm in our normal, day-to-day resting breathing pattern. In fact, in many cases the diaphragm becomes "frozen," showing little to absolutely no movement at all. In such a case it is maintained rigidly in place, and one breathes totally with the chest muscles.

There are a number of reasons why we develop poor breathing habits, just as there are a number of reasons we develop poor postural habits. Social and cultural conventions play a significant role. For example, women are told that flat stomachs are attractive, and they learn to hold their stomachs in. But by not allowing the stomach muscles to expand outward, they prevent the internal organs from moving out of the way in order that the diaphragm may flatten out. This freezes the diaphragm, forcing one to rely on chest breathing. Corsets, girdles and tight clothes also prevent the natural expansion of the abdominal cavity and interfere with

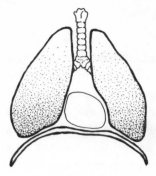

Figure 3
BLOOD DISTRIBUTION

The darker the area, the greater is the concentration of blood available for gas exchange.

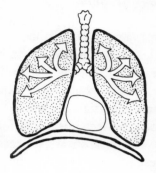

Figure 4
AIR FLOW INTO LUNGS DURING CHEST BREATHING

Chest wall expands, pulling lungs outward, creating a partial vacuum.

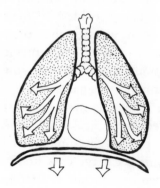

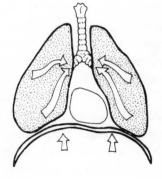

Figure 5
AIR FLOW INTO LUNGS DURING DIAPHRAGMATIC BREATHING

Diaphragm contracts and is pulled downwards (flat) creating a more complete vacuum, pulling air down into lowest lobes.

In exhalation, the diaphragm relaxes and is pushed back into a dome-shape, forcing air out of the lungs.

diaphragmatic breathing.

Men, on the other hand, are often told to puff their chests out, to "be a man." This is common in military training, but an exaggerated expansion of the chest interferes with diaphragmatic breathing and forces reliance upon the thoracic mechanism. Curiously enough, for military purposes (in which arousal is necessary and desirable) this inflated chest posture is quite appropriate. But for normal day-to-day functioning, a "macho" chest is not only dysfunctional—it also contributes to stress.

The psychological traumas we undergo as we grow up also contribute to the development of thoracic breathing. You can actually observe that fear tightens the stomach muscles, preventing diaphragmatic movement. For example, if you watch children when they are being scolded by their parents or other authority figures, you will see that their stomach muscles tighten, forcing them to rely on the thoracic mechanism. We all experience these small traumas as we grow up—and they have their effect on our breathing patterns.

Our posture, too, affects our breathing pattern. Most people do not sit properly, with their head, neck and trunk straight. Instead, they slouch or slump, with the spine curved out and a slight bend in the abdominal cavity. This totally prevents diaphragmatic movement, and again one must rely on thoracic breathing. In addition, poor posture does not allow the sympathetic and parasympathetic ganglianated cords to function properly, and this affects the entire system.

For these and many more reasons, we develop a habitual breathing pattern which results in increased stress and inefficient use of the cardiopulmonary system. On the other hand, diaphragmatic breathing reduces the work of the heart, and the whole system then begins to operate in a more re-laxed way. When there is an indication of coronary-vascular disease such as angina, diaphragmatic breathing is the one immediate step that can be taken in order to bring more oxygen to an overworked heart. But why wait until you have heart trouble?

Autonomic Functions and the Breath

As emotional imbalance disturbs the breathing pat-terns, shallow and jerky breathing also disturbs the mind. And when the mind is disturbed, the biochemistry is also affected. This can be examined easily. Simply pay attention to your breathing patterns, and you will discover that they change as your emotional states change. For example, when you are tense, or frightened, or angry, or concentrating, you will probably discover that you are unconsciously holding your breath or that there are pauses of different lengths between breaths. Similarly, when someone is depressed you will find that his breathing is very shallow and there are frequent sighs. Just as our mental/emotional states affect the way we breathe, the reverse is also true, for our breathing patterns and our emotional and physical states are intimately interrelated. Each affects and is affected by the other. For example, if you want a calm, steady mind, your breath must be calm and steady, without any noise, jerks, shallowness or prolonged pauses. In the Western world we are just beginning to explore this relationship.

The autonomic nervous system plays an important role in this area. Remember from chapter two that the right and left vagus nerves account for nearly eighty percent of parasympathetic nerve tissue, and these two parts of the vagus nerve pass through the thoracic cavity before joining the vital organs. The different motions of the chest cavity appear to stimulate the vagus nerve to either increase or decrease its activity, depending on the particular motion (and consequently the pressure) involved.

As Dr. Hymes points out in *Science of Breath*, thoracic (chest) breathing is directly related to activation of the fight-or-flight arousal mechanism, and that in times of danger, or when the organism needs to be aroused, breathing with both the diaphragm and the thoracic mechanism takes place. Thus one can utilize the lungs to their fullest capacity. But when there is no reason for activating the arousal mechanism, this full capacity is not needed. In fact, if one continues to utilize the lungs fully without there being any need for it, the entire physiology becomes imbalanced, and he will be under stress.

This is exactly what happens when we habitually breathe with the chest rather than with the diaphragm, for during thoracic breathing the motion of the lungs keeps the arousal mechanism activated. While the exact mechanism is still not clear, it looks as if the motions connected with chest breathing exert systematic pressure on the right vagus nerve—which in turn maintains a state of arousal. Whatever the mechanism, the consequence of thoracic breathing is to maintain a state of constant strain in the body and stress in the mind. In other words, as long as we breathe with the chest muscles instead of the diaphragm, we are continually creating an unnecessary level of stress. We are unable to relax.

To understand how our breath is related to autonomic balance, look at Figure 6 below. We see that inhalation

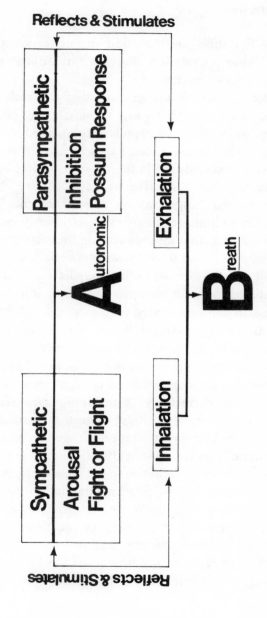

Figure 6

Breath and Autonomic Balance

directly but subtly reflects and stimulates sympathetic discharge, while exhalation directly but subtly reflects and stimulates parasympathetic discharge.

We can find many examples of this relationship. For instance, we notice that when we inhale there is an increase in heart rate, while exhalation is accompanied by a slowing of the heart. This phenomenon has been attributed to mechanical pressure exerted within the thoracic cavity, but it appears more likely that the efficient cause is the effect of the motion of the lungs on the activity of the vagus nerve.

Further indications of this relationship can be seen in the effects of autonomic activity on the respiratory patterns. For example, if one were to receive a sharp slap on the face, it would normally result in an immediate and strong sympathetic discharge as an instant arousal reaction. This would be reflected in the respiratory pattern as a quick inhalation, or gasp which would take place even if one were in the middle of an exhalation cycle when he was slapped.

On the other hand, strong parasympathetic states, such as depression, are characterized by sighs. No one ever speaks of a "gasp of depression." Other emotional states, such as anxiety or anger, also show disrupted breathing patterns. Because there is a direct relationship between inhalation and sympathetic activity, and exhalation and parasympathetic activity, an uneven, arhythmic air flow pattern (or respiratory motion) gives an uneven stimulation to sympathetic and parasympathetic discharge, resulting in autonomic imbalance—or stress. And by now you must know that habitual arrhythmic breathing patterns lead to habitual stress.

We can regulate the motion of the lungs through even breathing, and this leads to balanced autonomic functioning.

Thus, when one experiences stress, one can consciously make the inhalation and exhalation even and thus restore autonomic balance. Stress is not possible under these conditions.

Furthermore, specific manipulation of this relationship between breathing patterns and autonomic functioning can lead to predictable and controllable changes in levels of either arousal or relaxation. For example, the 2:1 breathing exercise (given at the end of this chapter), in which exhalation is twice as long as inhalation, provides a greater stimulus to parasympathetic discharge—and this leads to deep relaxation. This is the basis for the common practice of focusing on exhalation as a technique for inducing relaxation, but one should not exceed one's personal limits. One should always be comfortable when doing breathing exercises.

The flow of the breath (the smoothness and evenness of lung motion) can be measured on an instrument called the Cottle rhinomanometer. Here, one breathes into the nosepiece of the instrument, and this records a wave motion on a strip chart. The exhalation is measured above the base line, the inhalation below it. The ideal motion, or flow of respiration, looks like a sine wave—an even, smooth wave that indicates an even, uninterrupted flow of breath.

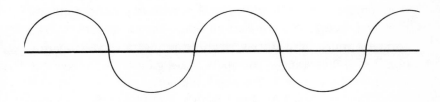

Researchers at the Himalayan Institute have found very few who even begin to approach this type of breath-flow pattern without proper training. Most people have patterns which differ dramatically from this ideal.

Preliminary research indicates that severe pathological states can be reflected in the wave patterns. For example, work by Dr. Maurice Cottle, an Ear, Nose and Throat specialist in Chicago, has shown that there is a distinctive wave pattern associated with heart attacks. This is characterized by what is called a mid-cycle rest, or pause; it looks like this:

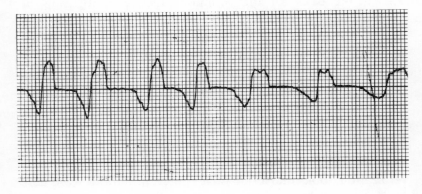

As shown in the simulated pattern above, the mid-cycle rest is a constant pause in the breathing pattern after the exhalation and before the inhalation. This, as we see below, is a form of apnea, and it may possibly reflect a very dangerous condition. The longer the pause, the greater is the danger. As we shall see later, this pause is a killer.

Chronic emotional states also appear to reflect characteristic wave patterns. For instance, one who suffers from anger often manifests a distinctive type of mid-cycle pause in which the pause is just after the inhalation and before the exhalation. The wave looks like this:

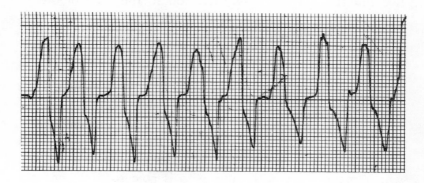

The effects of irregular breath-flow patterns are very subtle and often go unnoticed. However, careful observation of your own breath and the accompanying thoughts, feelings and sensations will bring them to awareness. For instance, if you watch yourself carefully, you will see that whenever there is a pause in your breathing, your thoughts change—and vice-versa. Consequently, if your breath is uneven and unstable it will be impossible for you to concentrate. Observe your breathing patterns closely. Do you breathe with your chest muscles? Are there any pauses or stops in your breath? By simple observation you will quickly be able to determine the kind of breathing habits you have. Is your breath uneven? Do you sigh a lot? Do you hold your breath and not breathe for periods of time?

As an experiment, simply concentrate on breathing diaphragmatically, making the inhalation and exhalation as smooth and even as possible. Picture in your mind your breath flowing exactly like the ideal wave form shown on page 181—no bumps, no pauses, no shakiness. Do this for five minutes, paying close attention to the flow of breath in and out of the nostrils. Then see how you feel both physically and mentally.

Also experiment during the day. The next time you are in a situation in which you are becoming angry or upset, concentrate a few moments on your breathing. Do diaphragmatic breathing, making your breath very even and steady. Then observe what happens to your feelings. You will notice that your ability to remain calm in the face of adversity is vastly improved. And there is no question but that the one who remains calm is the one who is able to think and act more creatively in any situation. Similarly, when you are feeling depressed or sad, observe how shallow your breathing has become. Then concentrate on diaphragmatic breathing and observe what happens to your mood.

Obviously it is important to regulate our breathing and eliminate the unevenness of our breath-flow pattern, and fortunately we can do this fairly easily. Since breathing can be either voluntary or involuntary, we can either forget about the breath, allowing the involuntary mechanisms to control the process, or we can take conscious control and impose another breathing pattern (habit) on it. The pattern we want to cultivate is even and diaphragmatic breathing.

While the intercostal muscles can control the movement of the chest cavity, they cannot adequately control the smoothness and evenness of the breath itself. Only the diaphragm can do this. So unless you alter the negative habit of constant thoracic breathing, you will never be able to control stress. Your own breathing will guarantee that you remain tense. And thus, through this one habit alone, we maintain constant stress.

Fortunately, it is not difficult to correct unhealthy breathing patterns. All that is required is a little daily practice. At the end of this chapter are several exercises which lead to the regulation and control of the breath, but before turning to them we must understand another area of the respiratory process. This too figures prominently in the body/breath/mind relationship; it too has an impact on autonomic functioning and the central nervous system.

The Nose—A Sophisticated Neurological Organ

The nose, surprisingly enough, is an extremely important organ in stress control, but most of us do not pay any attention to it unless there is some kind of difficulty such as postnasal drip, or congestion, or a sinus headache. In fact, many people breathe through the mouth and do not properly use the nostrils at all. In *Science of Breath* Dr. Ballentine points out that this may be a serious mistake for there are important neurological interconnections between the nose and the autonomic and central nervous systems.

The nasal passages occupy a unique position. The roof of the mouth forms the floor of the nasal cavity, and the roof of the nasal cavity forms part of the floor of the brain. Thus the nose is in a strategic position, for it is very near the nervous system and the pituitary gland. As a matter of fact, the first cranial nerve, the olfactory nerve, has endings in the uppermost part of the nasal cavity. When they are stimulated we receive direct input from the outside world to the most primitive part of the brain, the limbic system. This is considered to be the seat of the emotions in man and plays a vital role in regulating emotional states. The olfactory bulbs are a part of this system.

Within the nasal cavity are a series of structures which guide and direct the air as it flows in and out of the nostrils, and the most important are three seashell-like bulges which are called turbinates. They serve to baffle the air, to stir it up. Consequently, the air moving through the nostrils does not flow into the windpipe in a straight line, nor is the flow laminar. Instead, since it is forced to go through a series of winding, bending, looping, convoluting passageways, it is subjected to a great deal of turbulence.

Furthermore, the airways are not always open to the same degree, for the nasal passages are lined with erectile tissue (such as is found in the sexual organs) which can be engorged with blood and swell dramatically. This constantly alters the direction, or reshapes the flow, of air through the nasal passages in a cyclic process. Over a period of about two hours, for instance, the lining of one nostril will gradually become increasingly engorged until that nostril is almost completely blocked. Meanwhile, the lining shrinks in the other nostril, allowing that passage to become more open. In a healthy person this change of air flow shifts the breath from one nostril to the other over regular periods of time. Even more interesting is that this continuous shrinking and engorging forces air within the nostrils to be selectively altered (or shaped) into an infinite number of flow patterns.

The air flowing through the nasal passageway thus stimulates the nasal mucosa (the lining of the nose). Even when one is sitting quietly, the wind force in the narrow nasal passageways is approximately twenty miles an hour, and during heavy exertion the wind velocities can reach speeds of two hundred miles an hour. And this flow is all turbulence. The mucosa is saturated with nerve endings that connect with many parts of the nervous system, and it is these points of enural reflex that are stimulated by the turbulent air flow.

Changes in stimulation at these points of reflex can lead to changes in physiological processes elsewhere in the body. For instance, Sigmund Freud and Wilhelm Fliess, an Ear, Nose and Throat specialist, found that menstrual cramps were often related to an inflammation and discoloration of certain specific areas in the lining of the nose. When these were anesthetized, the menstrual pains would disappear until the effects of the anesthetic wore off.

The nasal passages also regulate the pressure of the air coming in and going out of the lungs. This may be measured, and it appears to produce the characteristic waveforms mentioned on page 181. As discussed earlier, these wave-forms also seem to reflect changes in physiological functioning that are, at first glance, not connected with the nasal passageways, or even with respiration.

The alterations, changes, pressures, stimulations, and rhythms of air through the nasal passages also appear to be connected to neurological functioning. Researchers who have studied this process think that everyone produces characteristic breathing patterns which can be indicative of certain physiological and emotional disorders (as was shown by Cottle's work mentioned earlier). This is in keeping with yoga teachings which state explicitly that breathing patterns are fundamental to regulating not only emotional, but also physiological states.

According to yoga science, for instance, the physiological effects associated with the air flow through the two nostrils are quite different. Interestingly enough, when research was conducted on discharge from the two nostrils, it was found that the electrical potential of the discharge was different for each nostril. While the implications of this difference are not fully understood, it does appear to confirm the experience of yoga science.

Furthermore, emotional states appear to be related to an overdominance of either right or left nostril activity. For example, preliminary research is beginning to indicate that some forms of depression are related to overactivity in the left nostril, while excessive air flow in the right nostril has been found to be associated with hyperactivity. This does not necessarily mean that the physical causes the mental (that a constantly overactive left nostril causes depression); it means simply that an overactive left nostril is interrelated with depression and an overactive right nostril is interrelated with hyperactivity.

Thus, in yoga therapy, one of the tools used for treating depression is a technique called alternate nostril breathing, a simple exercise designed to lead to autonomic balance. Alternate nostril breathing also corrects unhealthy respiratory patterns and expands the capacity of the lungs. Instructions for doing it are given on page 194, and it takes very little time to practice.

Furthermore, yoga science states that the right nostril should be made voluntarily active (dominant) when one is doing active work. Otherwise, the left nostril should be directed to be active. This conscious effort establishes the control of the mind over the breathing process. There is a more sophisticated technique used by the yogis, called the application of *sushumna*, by which they willfully direct both nostrils to flow freely at the same time. This is called *sandhi* or *sandhya*, and is a conscious state that helps to establish a calm mind.

To fully comprehend the subtle effects of the breath-flow cycle, however, requires profound study. There is only one ancient text available, *Swara Swarodayam*, which provides any detailed information on this subject. However, a competent teacher can play a vital role in teaching the student control over the process which is involved in the mind/body relationship.

It is interesting to note that students in the early stages of learning breath control need to use their fingers to exert pressure on the side of one nostril in order to increase the flow in the other nostril. As they develop their skill in concentration, however, they are able to control the flow of breath through concentration only. (This, incidentally, increases their powers of concentration.) Those who practice meditation systematically learn to apply *sushumna* (a state in which both nostrils are flowing freely) in order to attain a state of calm. In this way they voluntarily control their mental activities. As we shall see later, both breath awareness and meditation are of great therapeutic value in relieving and preventing stress.

Those who do not regulate their breathing during the day continue their irregular breathing habits during sleep—and snoring is one of the most potentially serious breathing problems we have. Although it is the focus of much joking, snoring may lead to a very dangerous condition—sleep apnea—for those with either known or unknown heart disease. Research indicates that if one snores with his mouth closed, the sound is created by the vibration of the uvula and is harmless. If, on the other hand, the mouth is open, the snoring sound is created by the collapsing of the larnyx—by a total relaxation of the muscles, which temporarily closes the air passageway. The breath flow is thus blocked, and one may not breathe for relatively long periods of time. This is thought to be a central nervous system dysfunction, and it is related to mouth breathing.

Dr. Alan Hymes, a thoracic surgeon who is currently researching sleep apnea and its relationship to heart attacks and mouth breathing, reports that when we stop breathing we create oxygen imbalances in the blood gases, thus creating a tremendous strain on the heart. While a variety of treatment modalities have been tried, particularly drugs, there has been little success in treating this potentially life-threatening condition. Dr. Hymes reports, however, that simply closing the mouth of the person who is snoring (thus forcing nasal breathing), corrects the sleep apnea—the snoring stops, the breath becomes even and steady, and chest breathing appears to change into diaphragmatic breathing. One's oxygen supply is thus increased, and the strain is off the heart. It is almost as if the stimulation of the nerve endings in the nasal mucosa is some kind of autonomic switch that restores respiratory balance and leads to diaphragmatic breathing.

Preliminary studies by Dr. Hymes have shown that over seventy-five percent of those who have heart attacks breathe through their mouth instead of through their nose. What is more, nearly all of those who habitually breathe through their mouth also snore; and of those who snore, eighty-four percent showed patterns of sleep and waking apnea lasting for periods of six to thirty seconds or longer. On the other hand, those who breathe through their nose exhibit little or no apnea.

Dr. Hymes suggests that it may be possible to "cure" apnea by retraining oneself to breathe diaphragmatically and through his nose. This not only relieves a very serious breathing problem, it also insures restful sleep. Consequently, one revitalizes the body, relieves stress and creates balance in the most "natural" way there is. This can happen. Deep, restful sleep can be brought about by practicing the proper breathing exercises. In other words, sleeping pills are not necessary if one regulates his breathing.

As you can see by now, direct, experiential knowledge of your own breathing is a necessary first step in learning to regulate the breath—and thus control stress. The second step is to practice a few exercises. They are not hard, and they take very little time, but the practice must be consistent in order to bring success. It is well worth the effort, however, for the easiest way to eliminate an unhealthy habit is to replace it with a healthy one.

Breathing Exercises

There are a number of breathing exercises that you can safely practice by yourself. They do not require a skilled teacher,* they are quite simple, and they do not require

---

* Since the breathing process is so intimately connected with neurological functioning, it is highly advisable that a beginning student not engage in advanced or rigorous breathing practices except under the guidance of a competent teacher. Breath retention should not be practiced under any circumstances unless one is being given expert instruction.

much time. They yield many benefits and are a necessary part of any effective stress management program. Following are five breathing exercises, a sleep exercise (which will alleviate insomnia), and directions for a nasal wash. Try them out for yourself.

Diaphragmatic Breathing

The purpose of this exercise is to reestablish diaphragmatic breathing as your normal, everyday moment-to-moment resting breathing habit. If you do no other exercise, be sure to practice this one. It is that important. It will be most effective if you practice at least three times a day for ten to fifteen minutes each time; eventually, the easy rhythmic motion of the diaphragmatic breathing will begin to replace the strained, unnatural chest breathing to which you have become habituated. You can speed the process by being aware of your breathing pattern as much as possible during the day, for the more aware of it you become, the more often you correct it (change from chest breathing to diaphragmatic breathing), and the faster you will replace thoracic with diaphragmatic breathing.

To Practice: Before you go to sleep and just after you wake up, place your right hand on your upper abdomen, with the little finger directly above the navel and the fingers spread so that the thumb is almost touching the chest. Place your left hand on the upper chest with the little finger between the two breasts. As you breathe, concentrate on the air moving down into the upper abdomen (as if you are filling your stomach with breath). The right hand should rise with the inhalation and fall with the exhalation; the left hand should not move. You should feel a slight motion in the lower portion of the chest cavity, but the upper portion should remain still. Within a few moments you will become more rested and quiet. Do not try to force the breath. Allow the motion to be gentle and effortless. Notice how easy it is to breathe deeply and easily, without any effort.

Benefits: This will lead to autonomic balance and a relaxed state, generally. After some weeks, depending on the individual, you will begin to notice subtle and gradual changes in your daily breathing patterns. Its movement will be more relaxed and rhythmic. As was discussed earlier, this leads to a greater efficiency of the pulmonary process and reduces the amount of work required for proper ventilation perfusion.

Even Breathing

While you are practicing diaphragmatic breathing, concentrate on making the breath very smooth and even. The inhalation and exhalation should be of the same length and have the same pressure. Do not exhale all the breath at the beginning of the exhalation. Concentrate on keeping the flow pressure even throughout the entire cycle. Eliminate all pauses, stops and shakiness in the breath, including the pause between inhalation and exhalation. Imagine that the breath is like a large wheel moving through the body without any pauses or stops. It is often helpful to picture the breath flow as a completely smooth, even sine wave (as discussed on page 181).

Benefits: The jerkier the breath, the more disruptive it is to the autonomic nervous system. When the breath is smooth and even, autonomic balance is achieved.

2:1 Breathing

After gaining control of diaphragmatic movement and establishing a smooth, even, rhythmic respiration, gently slow down the rate of exhalation until you are breathing out for about twice as long as you are inhaling. (It might be necessary to shorten the length of inhalation very slightly.) You are simply changing the rhythm of the breath. You are not trying to fill the lungs completely nor empty them completely. You are only altering the motion of the lungs in a very systematic way. You may count six on the exhalation and three on the inhalation, or eight on the exhalation and four on the inhalation—or whatever is most comfortable for you. Then, after you have established this gentle rhythm, stop the mental counting and focus on the smoothness and evenness of the breath flow. Eliminate all jerks and pauses. Maintain 2:1 diaphragmatic breathing for as long as you wish.

Benefits: 2:1 breathing establishes a relaxed state in the body by very subtly stimulating the parasympathetic system more than the sympathetic system. This leads to relaxation and reduces arousal in the body even if you do it only a few moments.

Alternate Nostril Breathing

This is one of the most important breathing exercises available. Its purpose is to increase the capacity of the lungs as well as to increase one's control over the breathing process and the autonomic system. It is also very useful in developing one's power of concentration. It should be practiced three times daily, and it will take only a few minutes to do.

To Practice: Sit comfortably, with your head, neck and trunk in alignment (the back should be straight but allow for the natural S curve of the spine). Rest the index and middle fingers of the right hand on the space between the two eyebrows. Determine which nostril is active. (The active nostril is the one in which the air is flowing freely. The passive nostril is the nostril in which there is some natural blockage due to the natural cyclic swelling of the mucosa.) If the right nostril is active, press your ring finger against the left nostril, closing it, and gently exhale through the right nostril, counting to six (or about six seconds) mentally as you exhale. Then inhale immediately through the same nostril for a count of six.

Now press the thumb gently against the right nostril, closing it off, and at the same time release the pressure on the left nostril. Exhale for a count of six, and then inhale for a count of six through the left nostril.

Now press the ring finger gently against the left nostril, closing off the flow, and at the same time release the pressure from the thumb on the right nostril. Exhale for a count of six, and inahle for a count of six through the right nostril.

Close the right nostril and open the left. Exhale and inhale for a count of six in the left nostril. Close the left nostril and open the right. Exhale and inhale to counts of six in the right nostril. Close the right nostril and open the left. Exhale and inhale for counts of six through the left nostril. This completes the exercise. You have just done three rounds.

In this case we started with the right nostril. Begin with whichever nostril is active. The entire exercise consists simply of exhaling and inhaling through the active nostril and then through the passive nostril and repeating this procedure two more times. There are only six complete breaths in the exercise, three on each side.

After three rounds of alternate nostril breathing, bring your hand down and slowly resume your normal breathing. Focus as much attention as possible to the flow of the breath during the exercise. When there are no bumps, jerks or pauses, and when the flow is evenly distributed throughout the entire cycle, then increase the length of the breath (go from a count of six to a count of eight). Begin with a count which is comfortable and concentrate on making the breath smooth and even at this length. It is the smoothness of the flow which is important here, not how long you can make your breath. Length will increase as your control over the flow increases.

Benefits: This exercise not only regulates the respiratory patterns, it also develops control over mental states, for balancing the cyclic rhythm of nostril flow appears to balance hemispheric functioning in the brain. This exercise also leads to increased lung capacity and, as mentioned above, to a greater degree of control over concentration.

The Complete Breath

In this exercise all three mechanisms of inhalation—diaphragmatic, thoracic and clavicular (collarbones) are brought into use. Inhale first, using the diaphragm and expanding the belly; then continue the inhalation by expanding the chest; then let the inhalation continue to the very top of the lungs at which point a slight upward movement of the clavicles may be experienced. The exhalation is done in reverse motion, letting the clavicles drop slightly, then letting the chest wall collapse slightly, then letting the belly collapse as the diaphragm moves upward, pushing the air out of the lungs. The breath should be slow and smooth, without any pauses or jerks.

This complete breath is a very useful technique to use when you are sitting at your desk and feel a lot of tension in your shoulders. A five-minute practice will be very helpful in reducing not only muscle tension but also mental fatigue.

Sleep Exercise

Breathing is a key element in relaxation, and this exercise uses your breathing process to help you get to sleep. It will also help you sleep more restfully. The following steps make up the exercise. Follow them closely:

1. All breathing is 2:1. Exhale for twice as long as you inhale.

2. Use a comfortable count such as 6:3 or 8:4. You are not trying to completely empty or fill the lungs. The 2:1 ratio should be effortless.

3. Pay close attention to your breath. There should be no stops, pauses or shakiness during either the inhalation or the exhalation. Eliminate even the pause between inhalation and exhalation.

The exercise goes as follows:

8 breaths lying on your back
16 breaths lying on your right side
32 breaths lying on your left side

Very few people are able to finish this exercise.

The Nasal Wash

For healthy nasal passages, a daily nasal wash with saline solution is extremely helpful. This simple, easy wash will alleviate many nasal congestion problems and will help keep the nasal passages free from excess mucus. It will also facilitate the breathing exercises.

To Practice: As a part of your morning wash, fill a regular kitchen glass (eight ounces) with lukewarm tap water. Add approximately one eighth teaspoon of salt. (The water should be about as salty as tears. If it is too salty, it will sting; if it is not salty enough, it will create an unpleasant pressure inside the nose). Bring the glass up to the nostrils, tilting the head back. Slowly sniff the water into the nostrils, then drop your head and let the water drain back out. You may choke slightly the first time or two, but you will quickly learn how to close off your throat.

After a little practice you will be able to tilt your head back and to one side. Then bring the water in through the upper nostril and let it drain out the lower. This will cleanse and rejuvenate the mucus membrane lining the inside of the nostrils. After a little more practice, you will be able to take the water through both nostrils, down into the throat and out the mouth. This will cleanse the entire passageway.

Benefits: This wash cleanses and rejuvenates the mucous membrane, alleviating congestion and helping to prevent infections in the sinus area. It thus helps eliminate the pain of sinus headaches. It also helps reduce the symptoms of allergies as well as helps prevent colds and other minor infections of the mucous membrane. Don't be afraid of this wash. Try it for a week before forming any opinion about its usefulness.

Meditation: Pathway to Freedom

Meditation is the art of living and being in the world. In modern technologically advanced societies, man is still searching for meaning and fulfillment. We realize that we cannot retreat to some isolated place or create some long-lost Utopia in order to find tranquility and peace of mind. We must find a way by which we can function within our society—a way in which we can fulfill our social obligations and yet retain our balance.

Man is really a citizen of two worlds, his inner reality and his external reality. He is both consciously and unconsciously making efforts to create a bridge between these two. But pressures from the external world, the many social and economic pressures of day-to-day life, create disturbances in his inner reality, and his balance is upset.

There is a method for creating this bridge successfully so that one may participate fully in modern life. This is meditation. *Meditation* is not a religious word; it has no religious connotations. It is a practical, systematic method which allows one:

To understand himself at all levels of being
To understand his environment completely
To eliminate and prevent inner conflicts
To obtain a tranquil and peaceful mind

Our internal reality can be controlled when we learn to become physically very still and very quiet, for when we learn to breathe with the diaphragm, serenely and deeply, we release our physical and nervous tension. After experiencing the benefits of the breathing exercises, we are spontaneously led to understand the various functions of our mind. No one else can do this for us. We first come in touch with the thoughts and images of the conscious mind, that part of the mind we use during the waking state. Then, as we learn to consciously let go of all the images passing through our mental train, we acquire the habit of witnessing the thought patterns, themselves. In this way we directly experience, and thus come to know, the nature of our own mind.

Through this direct experience we understand that the habit of the mind is to identify itself with the objects and experiences of the world, as reflected in our thoughts and emotions. And it is this which creates serious problems for us. When we learn to witness this thinking process, however, but not identify with it, we have access to the unconscious mind.

This is a vast reservoir of symbols, ideas, thoughts, emotions, desires and motivations; as we continue to develop a strong sense of observation, we find that we are able to break our identification with these deep thoughts and images, too, and we no longer suffer from the sense of identity with them which is a perpetual source of stress. Our mind, our inner reality, is then in balance, and our mastery over stress on all levels—physical, mental and emotional—is complete. The method for doing this is called meditation. It is the systematic way by which we gain freedom from stress.

Meditation is for those who want to live fully in the world, to enjoy it and yet remain unaffected by the rush and roar of modern life. Learning to perform our tasks and duties and yet be free from external pressures is a specific technique called *meditation in action*. When we understand and utilize this form of meditation, we remain calm and composed no matter what kind of pressures are exerted from the external environment.

Meditation is effective because it eliminates the greatest cause of stress—loneliness. We usually think of loneliness as wanting or needing to have some relationship with another person, but this is only a superficial symptom of the real thing. The lonely person is one who does not know himself, and thus he does not know his purpose in life. So the most important goal of life remains unknown.

Clinical experience has shown that the most important source of emotional distress is not knowing oneself. This should not be surprising since we are taught from childhood on to search, examine and verify the possibilities of happiness only in the external world. But no one teaches us how to serach, examine and verify our inner reality. Thus, the most important facet of our life remains unknown to us. Our lack of training makes us insecure, for we remain dependent on our relationship to people and objects in the external world for our happiness and fulfillment. A series of expectations remain lurking in our hearts and minds which creates constant stress—and this is the primary source of suffering.

Focusing on the mere material goals of life distracts us from our inner reality as well. And to remain obsessed with the external world leads us to the second greatest source of stress—our fears of the unknown. When we begin to confront these fears, however, through meditation, they all vanish, and we begin to realize that fear is mostly imaginary. Then, as our fears begin to vanish, we discover the source of strength which is already within us.

As we know, all of our habits, both the good and the bad, are formed in the unconscious mind, and as long as our identity remains locked to them, we will not be in control of ourselves. With gradual, continuous effort in meditation, however, we can learn to go beyond these habits and experience the source of our inner strength which can be called the center of consciousness. And once we are able to attain this state of mind, we become free from all stress.

Misperceptions About Meditation

Most of us have, at best, a fragmentary knowledge of what meditation really is, for much of the material written about it is incomplete and distorted. For instance, meditation is often confused with rituals, philosophies and practices which have nothing to do with the process. So before discussing what meditation is, it may be helpful to first examine some of the more common misconceptions.

One of the most common mistakes is to confuse meditation and religion. Meditation is not a religion, nor is it connected with any particular philosophy. It is, however, a tool that has been utilized by all major religions and, for that matter, by agnostics and athiests as well. Meditation is a personal technique for increasing internal awareness. Just as cleaning your body has nothing to do with your religious belief, neither does cleansing your mind (which is part of the process of meditation).

Likewise, meditation has no intrinsic link with any particular culture. Meditative processes are found in all areas of the world. Eastern methods of meditation, however, particularly the yoga system, have been more completely and systematically developed than others, and thus they often serve as models for the process. This is like saying that American technology has served as a model for development in Eastern countries, which is also true. But technology, like meditation, is a tool and does not belong to any particular country, culture or religion. Using technology does not turn the user into an American, nor does the use of meditation turn one into a Hindu, or a Zen monk, or an Indian or a yogi.

Meditation is not a form of hypnosis either, but they do share one basic characteristic—one must be relaxed to do either one. There the similarity stops. In order to be hypnotized, one must focus one's attention on a suggestion (either your own or the hypnotist's) and comply with it. Most of us are already hypnotized, as a matter of fact, in the sense that we are always following somebody's suggestions (we prefer to call it peer pressure, or advertising).

Meditation, on the other hand, is a state of observation; it is not following anything at all. Concentration on a single point such as the breath, or a *mantra* should not be confused with suggestion, for suggestion implies action taken. Observation means only observing—there is no judgment or action. The difference between suggestion and observation is like the difference between watching a particular horse (observation) and getting up on the horse and riding away with it (hypnosis). They are two different actions, having two different outcomes.

In hypnosis you surrender your own control to the suggestion. In meditation you expand conscious self-control and awareness. What is more, recent research indicates that one sustains no significant changes, either physically or psychologically, after the long-term practice of hypnosis.* On the other hand, those who practice some form of meditation over a period of time experience significant reductions in the physiological parameters of stress and increased psychological maturity. While there are new induction techniques leading to states that appear to approach the meditative state, if suggestion is followed, it is still hypnosis and thus limited in scope and power. Only when the subject changes his perspective from involvement with the hypnotic suggestion to pure observation can meditation take place.

Meditation is definitely not compatible with drug usage, either. While there are many so-called "teachers" who advocate the use of psychedelic drugs to supplement meditation, this is because they are ignorant of the meditative process. Certain drugs are said to "expand" consciousness, but this is more like an explosion than an expansion, and the collapse of awareness which inevitably follows the explosion

* Changes resulting from hypnosis are specific to the hypnotic suggestion only, and are not lasting. This includes the use of hypnosis as a part of therapy, for in this case hypnotherapy is part of the overall process that induces personality change.

leads to confusion rather than clarity. Meditation, on the other hand, is the systematic, controlled expansion of consciousness that takes place totally under one's own control. Drugs are antithetical to the development of self-control and lead ultimately to internal chaos, so beware of the "easy" way to consciousness-expansion. The consequences are inevitably an increase in suffering rather than an increase in understanding.

A last misconception to clear up is that meditation does not require one to change one's life style. Any change that takes place as the result of meditation will be organic and due to increased psychological growth and maturity. There is no meditative profession or life style, but there are life styles which will prevent one from meditating. (These also prevent one from growing in any direction.) Meditation is as useful to the executive as it is to the plumber, as it is to the housewife, as it is to the student. To repeat, meditation is a tool; it is not a way of life. Everyone can benefit from it. Not everyone will (or can) utilize the same form of meditation, but there are many different methods—and they all work. The tool can be adapted to any personality, at any time, in any reasonable life style. After all, awareness is not prejudicial.

Components of Meditation—Relaxation

Relaxation is often confused with meditation, but it is not the same thing; it is only the first step toward meditation. It is a very important step, however, for without physical and mental relaxation the mind cannot concentrate, and if there is no concentration there is no meditation. Relaxation also deepens as a result of meditation, particularly the form of meditation which is called concentrative, or exclusive, meditation in which the more the mind become focused, the greater is the natural physiological response of relaxation. This occurs quite naturally and spontaneously. In fact there is no real relaxation unless the mind does become focused.

What is more, meditation is not necessarily associated with any particular brain-wave pattern. Alpha waves are associated with relaxation, but you can meditate while producing any kind of pattern—beta, alpha, theta, and even delta. The psychological states of reverie produced during alpha and theta waves are also not meditation. They are generally desirable states, possibly associated with creativity, but meditation is not any psychological state; it is a process which leads to another complete level of consciousness which is different from the levels with which we are familiar —waking, dreaming and sleeping. It is a state of high potential energy which is focused, not scattered in "nervous energy," random thoughts and feelings, or body tension.

The steps leading to meditation—relaxation and concentration—are also very effective stress-management techniques. In stress management, for instance, relaxation reduces the levels of already-existing stress and gives the body a rest. This is particularly important for those whose autonomic system is imbalanced on the side of sympathetic arousal. In such cases the consistent practice of relaxation techniques is necessary to keep chronic stress levels from rising and to teach one the skill of "tuning down" the arousal mechanism. For those suffering from a possum response, however, relaxation is generally not a useful tool. The body is already tuned down to an extreme degree. Consequently, we must understand that relaxation is only a part of effective stress mangement just as it is only a part of meditation. It is not the whole key.

There are various methods of relaxation. Some emphasize the body and control it through imagery. These are helpful, particularly for beginners, but the deepest relaxation is achieved through control of the breath and breath awareness. Diaphragmatic breathing, alternate nostril breathing, 2:1 breathing and the other exercises provided at the end of the previous chapter are the best methods for inducing controlled relaxation, and they will restore autonomic balance without producing an overrelaxed state which leaves the body and mind both drowsy. Whatever technique you use, it should be systematic so that you quickly develop your skill. When you have done this, relaxation should never take longer than five minutes. With constant practice you can learn to relax in only a few breaths.

Components of Meditation—Inner Concentration

After calming the body, the next step is to calm and focus the mind through inner concentration. This is another component of meditation that is often mistaken for the whole. In truth, however, inner concentration is the stage before meditation, and if properly developed it leads to meditation.*

Most of us have the ability to concentrate to some

---

* Most of the research on "meditative" states has really been made on inner concentration, not meditation. This does not deny the usefulness of the research; it only points out an incomplete state of knowledge about meditation.

degree, but it is nearly always limited to an object or situation in the external world. That is, we can concentrate on our work, our play, or a book, but if we have to concentrate on an internal process, we quickly find that we have little capacity for it. Our attention flows easily to the external world, but it strongly resists attempts to redirect the flow inward. It seems as if anything in the external world can disrupt inward-focused attention, a result of our education and training being geared toward focusing on the external world of facts, figures and objects. We are taught to study the objects of our senses but not the filter mechanism—the mind in which that sensory data is collected, organized and given meaning.

As a result, when we try to concentrate on some inner event we find that our attention is constantly being pulled here and there by competing thoughts and feelings, and we seem to have very little conscious control over them. Usually we cannot even choose not to think about things that bother us unless we suppress or repress them. If we are involved in a situation that is fearful for us, our minds keep returning to the problem, over and over, and this generates more fear. When we want to sleep, our minds create a continuous stream of thoughts that prevent us from doing so. The harder we try to focus, the more insistent the disturbances become.

Many times we find someone who seems to have it all together, who appears to be calm and steady, but as we come to know him better we discover that internally he is a raging emotional storm. If we are really honest, we will admit that this is true of all of us to some degree. Very few of us have the capacity to truly control the mind, to have inner tranquility and calmness. Very few of us have the ability to focus the mind on one inner object—a thought, an image or a sound.

The importance of being able to do this will be evident if we remember that stress is created by the way we perceive and interpret external events. It is our own thoughts and emotional processes which create it, for the body is programmed by the images in our mental processes. If these remain uncontrolled, then our stress remains uncontrolled. This does not mean that we are suppressing or repressing our thoughts, however. Real control is the ability to consciously choose which thoughts we think and to choose how we utilize our emotional states. It is the ability to choose our responses through controlling the inner dialogue of the mind.

In order to gain this control, in order to be able to consciously calm the mind and free it from disturbances, we must be able to concentrate inwardly, to be able to focus our attention on the point we consciously choose, not on the points chosen by our unconscious habits or strong emotions. This is the first step in developing awareness of, and control over, the subtle habits of the mind. Then by focusing the attention on one thought, image or sound, gradually all others are brought under control and become quiet.

An analogy between the mind and a deep lake is often used to clarify this process. When there are many waves and ripples, the surface of the lake is disturbed, but when all of these are brought together into one wave, the lake becomes calm and clear. The calmer the lake, the deeper one can see into it. Likewise, when all thoughts, images and sensations are emerged into one thought, image or sensation (through focusing the attention on one point), then the mind becomes calm and clear and we are able to increase our awareness of the events which lie deeper in the mind.

In other words, the purpose of inner concentration is to expand our internal awareness. Another way of understanding this is to picture the mind as a very large, very hard block of ice. Something is buried in the center that we want to see directly, but to get at it we need to break through the ice. If we take a flat, wide board and beat on the ice, it will take a long time to break through. Our effort is dispersed over the flat surface, and we have very little power to penetrate the hard ice. On the other hand, if we use a sharp ice pick so that all the force of the blow is focused on a single point, we can very quickly break through to see the buried object directly.

It is the same with the mind. Our attention is usually so scattered that we cannot penetrate the unconscious. As with the flat board, our force of effort is too dispersed to have much effect. Our will is dissipated by constant interruptions, worries, desires, sensations, fancies and fantasies— and all the other activities that go on in the mind and body. Consequently we have very little knowledge about our total mind.

We speak of our unconscious mind as if it were a permanent reality, as if there were no way to directly apprehend, or perceive (and thus no way to understand) it. Psychiatry has instilled in us a fear of the unconscious that is both unreasonable and ill-founded, for in reality "unconscious" simply means that we haven't paid attention. Our so-called unconscious mind is not out of reach of conscious awareness. We can indeed begin to know our total mind, with all of its habits and talents, if we train our attention to penetrate this vast area. This is the task of inner concentration and meditation.

To do this we need a focal point for our mind. Breath awareness is not only the simplest, most direct way of developing inner concentration, it also leads to balance in the autonomic nervous system. When this happens, you not only have control over stress, you also develop conscious mastery over both your physiological processes and your emotional events.

Is this difficult? The hardest thing is to remember to be aware of the breath. All you need to do is simply direct your awareness to the base of the bridge between the two nostrils and concentrate on the slight feeling of coolness as the air flows in and the warmth as the air flows out. Do not think about the breath; just concentrate on the feeling as it flows in and out of the nostrils. Do not be concerned if you cannot detect warmth, or even coolness. That sensitivity will develop as you practice. Remember—you are not trying to control the breath nor are you trying to analyze or conceptualize about the flow of the breath. No thinking! Focus only on the feeling. And remember—the more relaxed you are, the easier this will be.

As you do this, notice what happens to the stream of thoughts inside the mind. As you will see, it is stopped. No more chatter! You cannot feel the breath and have that stream of thoughts at the same time. You have turned the thinking faculty off by focusing on the perceptual faculty. In psychological terms, you have moved from a cognizing, categorizing, abstracting mode of being to a more pristine perceptual mode. And there are some very important consequences of this change.

The first, and one that you will sense immediately, is

that your body becomes more relaxed. This is a natural and inevitable response of the body as the mind becomes calm and centered, for since there are no more thoughts going on, the body is not responding to any directions or imagery. Thus, activation of the body is substantially reduced. You will also notice, as you attend to the feeling of the breath, that it naturally becomes very smooth and even. This has a further relaxing effect on the body.

Then, as you continue to practice, you will notice that you tend to stay more relaxed and calm during the day. In other words, the more often you are aware of your breath, the more calm and relaxed the other times of the day will be. Your thinking will become increasingly clear. In fact, one very useful practice is to concentrate on the breath for a few moments, allowing the body to breathe evenly and diaphragmatically, before working with any troublesome problem. You will find that your ability to work with the problem is enhanced because you have focused your attention; the mind is no longer bothered with trivia.

Increased perceptual awareness also develops as a result of breath awareness, for by halting the flow of thoughts you have an opportunity to pay more attention to perceptual data. For example, the next time you are listening to someone, practice breath awareness. Normally we continue to keep on thinking when we are listening to someone else talk to us. We are answering them mentally, or even thinking about something else altogether. But if you pay attention to the feeling of the breath when listening, you will be surprised at how much more you actually hear in that person's voice. You are not, however, increasing your perceptions; you are gradually learning how to attend to the great mass of perceptual data which is already there! The first few times you do this it may seem a bit strange to you, but soon you will notice an increased awareness.

There is, however, no alternative to sitting quietly and very still if one is to develop the power of inner concentration. A systematic method is given below. It is best not to spend more than five minutes on preliminary relaxation exercises. If you become skilled at relaxation, you will be able to devote most of your time to training your power of inner concentration. This will lead to deeper relaxation, and as the mind is gradually trained to go where you consciously direct it, your ability to control and eliminate stress increases. More important, as you increase your capacity for concentration, you are preparing yourself to use the most sophisticated tool for self-knowledge and self-control available—meditation.

Meditation: Pathway to Freedom

Meditation is the only process by which awareness is systematically expanded (or increased) under one's direct control. The word meditation should not be a noun, but a verb; it is a process. It is not a state; it is, rather, the means through which we can achieve a particular level of awareness. According to yoga, it is a highly refined technical term. *Meditation is a continuous stream of effortless concentration, on a single point, over an extended period of time.*

The phrase *continuous stream* indicates that in meditation there is an uninterrupted flow of concentration. The attention never wavers or wanders. Remember that pauses and stops in the breath actually reflect pauses and halts in the mental processes. That is, uneven breathing means uneven attention in the mind. So it should be obvious that the entire process of meditation is directly related to an even, steady flow of breath. In other words, in order for concentration to flow evenly, without pause, the breath must flow evenly, without pause. Those who have not controlled the breath through diaphragmatic breathing and breath awareness cannot yet practice meditation. *Even, steady breath leads to even, steady inner concentration—and this leads to meditation.*

The next two terms *effortless concentration* define the quality of the concentration. It means exactly that—the flow of concentration must be effortless, without any struggle. If there is a struggle with the mind, if you are trying to make the mind concentrate, or if you are using willpower, it is not meditation. For example, when you are concentrating on the breath and suddenly your mind begins to wander off, and you immediately restrain the mind and bring your attention back to the breath, the very effort required to refocus the concentration keeps what you are doing from being meditation. Meditation is not thinking about meditation; it is the process of the concentration flow itself. The word *effortless* also points to another difference between concentration and meditation, for concentration evolves into meditation when the faculty of attention is so highly trained that effort is no longer required to focus it.

The next phrase *on a single point* means that the mind does not wander here and there but remains focused on the object of observation. This is a bit more difficult than you might suspect. Try for a few moments to concentrate on only the word *blue*. What happens? If you observe carefully, you will perceive all sorts of thoughts come into your mind, associations based upon the word *blue.* Or you might have felt an itch somewhere on your body, or moved in order to get more comfortable. All of these events, and many more, are continually there to distract the mind. So single-minded, one-pointed concentration is a skill that must be consistently practiced over a period of time before one has mastery over one's wandering mind.

This phrase also differentiates between meditation and contemplation, for in contemplation one focuses on a word or concept and then attempts to understand and experience it in all its aspects. The mind is trained to fully understand its core meaning as well as all its relational meanings. In the meditaton process, on the other hand, all relational (and, of course, non-relational) aspects of the object of concentration are purposefully and systematically excluded. One does not "think about" anything. One focuses on it, and concentration is one-pointed.

Finally the phrase *over an extended period of time* indicates that the flow of effortless, uninterrupted and one-pointed concentration must be more than momentary. Concentration must be unbroken and maintained. This is difficult; even two or three minutes of it is quite an accomplishment.

Thus, as one develops his power of inner concentration, it will slowly extend itself into meditation. The process is evolutionary. In other words, one does not practice meditation; one practices inner concentration, and when that inner concentration becomes effortless, unbroken and sustained, then one is in meditation. There will be no question about whether or not you are meditating; the process will be complete in and of itself. You will know the difference through your own experience.

The Method

The practice of meditation should be done very systematically. Choose a quiet, clean and well-ventilated room, and choose a time when you will be undisturbed and free from your essential duties. Sit in a comfortable posture (on a straight chair, or cross-legged on a firm pillow on the floor) with the head, neck and trunk straight (this allows for the natural S curve of the spine). The essential points are that your posture is straight and comfortable.

Spend the first few moments practicing the alternate nostril breathing exercise (given in chapter six). Then breathe diaphragmatically and evenly through the nostrils. Determine not to be disturbed by the mind. When you are as relaxed as you can be, concentrate on the feeling of the breath at the base of the bridge of the nose between the two nostrils. Concentrate on feeling the flow of breath through both nostrils.

Then on an inhalation, bring your focus of concentration to either the space between the two eyes, the pineal center, or to the space between the two breasts, the cardiac plexus. If you are more intellectual than emotional, you should center your focus on the pineal center. If you are more emotional than intellectual, you should focus your concentration on the cardiac plexus. This concentration or focus should be on the space within the body, not on the surface skin area. Then allow your thoughts to flow without interruption, and develop the sense of being a witness to the thoughts.

Sit for as long as you comfortably can, letting your own capacity be the determining factor. But do so on a daily basis, for regularity is necessary in order for you to increase your capacity. It will also help if you select a specific time, and do your practice at that time every day. This helps establish the habit of sitting to meditate, and this time becomes associated with a relaxed, peaceful state of mind.

To develop the skill of inner concentration (which evolves into meditation) the mind must first become still and calm. To accomplish this requires consistent daily practice—sitting quietly, closing the eyes and bringing full attention to the flow of the breath, then to a particular center, and then observing the flow of thoughts and images. To develop this skill of observation, a single focus point is chosen to develop the power of inner concentration.

For this reason *mantras* are used in many great traditions around the world. A *mantra* is a syllable, sound, word or set of words, which are specifically prescribed according to the student's nature. It calms the mind and allows one's conscious awareness to penetrate into the deeper levels of the mind at a gentle, controlled rate. This penetration, in turn, opens new channels of knowledge by leading the mind to a higher level of consciousness. Thus, through concentration, we can experience the source of our inner strength, the center of consciousness, and we are then able to fully utilize our true potential.

Care is needed in choosing the focal point because many can lead to negative states. The importance of this will be obvious when we examine the consequences of much of the inner concentration that is not under our control. For instance, there are many people who naturally concentrate on sensations. Unfortunately, this can lead to such problems as hypochondria. In the same vein, an anxiety neurotic concentrates on thoughts, but they are the kind that create problems rather than help him train his attentional faculty. Still others concentrate on certain images and become fearful. Thus, the particular object of concentration must be chosen with great care.

The practice given above—developing a sense of witnessing the flow of thoughts—is an excellent beginning exercise. This can be refined and expanded with the help of a competent teacher, one who is knowledgeable in all aspects of meditation, including breathing exercises, and who practices these techniques himself.

The Two Forms of Meditation

There are two basic forms of meditation—inclusive and exclusive—which are like the two sides of a coin. These terms are merely for categorical convenience, as both involve concentration and observation. The difference lies in the objects of awareness. For instance, in the concentrative, or exclusive, form of meditation all objects such as thoughts, images, sensory impressions and feelings, are eliminated except one (such as the feeling of breath or a *mantra*). This is the popularly-known form of meditation, the one most familiar to the lay person—and it takes place when one is sitting quietly with the eyes closed.

In the other form of meditation, one-pointedness is focused upon the stream of consciousness itself. No object, perception, thought, feeling or image is excluded. In other words, all the movements in the mind are included in the observational field, but the point of observation is total non-identification with the ongoing events whether they be internal mental or physical objects (thoughts or feelings) or external processes. All are noted with the same neutral equanimity that one would experience when watching the flow of water under a bridge. One-pointedness is fixed on the flow itself. When the observational state is interrupted by involvement (identification) with an object in the flow, then concentration is broken. This is often called meditation in action, and it can be done as one performs one's daily tasks.

Both forms of the meditative process require the consistent practice of inner concentration before they will evolve into meditation. Both are necessary for the development of self-knowledge. The two forms are complementary; each enhances the other, and each makes the other easier. They both lead to greater awareness of the subtle inner processes of the subconscious mind, and by practicing both one greatly speeds up the overall process of increased self-control.

Meditation and Stress Management

As we have already discussed, *Meditation is the systematic expansion of personal conscious awareness for the purpose of gaining increased experiential knowledge of our true inner potential*, for meditation provides a wide variety of benefits from the most mundane to the most spiritual. For some, it will provide physical relaxation, for others it is a method for achieving tranquility. Whatever the reason for doing so, if one meditates one gradually eliminates those habits and patterns that result in pain, discomfort and suffering. The benefits begin immediately. You do not have to be a great meditator to experience them, and the more you put into your practice, the more you gain from it.

In terms of stress management, inner concentration and meditation are the keys to freedom. It is true that a consistent practice of relaxation and physical exercises will modify or alleviate stress, but they will not eliminate the stress-inducing patterns in the mind. Doing only relaxation and physical exercises is like putting out a fire—only to come back and find it burning again. It is more efficient to remove the conditions which create the fire than it is to continually have to put the fire out. In other words, it is much simpler and more effective to understand the subtle mental/emotional origins of stress, and then to alter or remove them, than it is to continually rescue the body and mind from stress.

This can be achieved only through the consistent practice of inner concentration and meditation. What happens is that through concentration we become aware of, and alter, the subtle inner processes, and these alterations in turn affect and alter not only the thought and emotional patterns, but also bodily and behavioral responses. These changes evolve from the center of one's being outward and result in a gradual transformation of the entire personality.

This is the great value of meditation. It enhances and promotes our evolutionary growth process, and since this takes place as a natural consequence of our own effort, it remains under our control. It is altogether different from change imposed by the external environment, for when we meditate no person, therapy, drug or event imposes change upon us. We need only to make the internal effort to enhance and guide our own innate capacity for growth.

A number of specific benefits result directly from inner concentration and meditation. For instance, physiologically, we are able to enter into very profound states of relaxation, for when the mind becomes concentrated on one point, the body becomes deeply relaxed. Furthermore, when one meditates there is a gradual change in the physiology of the body reflecting a significant and permanent reduction of stress—slower pulse rate, a lower and more stable blood pressure, a more stable galvanic skin response, deeper and more even breathing patterns as well as lower blood lactate levels. These all have an obvious and positive effect on our physical and mental health.

But this change in physiological stress is only a reflection (and a consequence) of more subtle changes in one's psychology, for just as physical stress is reduced by the practice of meditation, so also is psychological stress and/or anxiety. Then, since one's mind is no longer focusing and brooding upon anticipated threats or remembered pain, one becomes less anxious and fearful, psychologically, and consequently the instructions from the cortex to the hypothalamus do not activate either the fight-or-flight response or the possum response. Moreover, as one meditates there is a corresponding increase in self-confidence and self-acceptance, for research indicates that those who practice consistently increase in measures of self-actualization (an indication of increasing maturity).

Finally, this growing maturity is reflected in one's behavior. Meditators experience less need for (and use less) alcohol and drugs of all types—prescribed and nonprescribed. In addition, their life becomes more relaxed and stable and more under their conscious control. In addition, compulsive and rigid behavior (which results in negative consequences) is slowly given up and replaced by more helpful behavior. For instance, compulsive eating habits, smoking and compulsive talking are gradually modified and eliminated when one meditates regularly. All of these changes take place when internal, psychological health is improved. In general, then, we can say that any unwanted, stress-induced behavior undergoes gradual alteration when one consistently practices meditation. This is inevitable.

The development of inner concentration also leads to some very important and useful skills. First of all, by increasing our ability to concentrate inwardly we are also increasing our capacity for concentration on external factors. Instead of letting our attention wander here and there, we are more able to concentrate on the work at hand, thus increasing our effectiveness and reducing the amount of nonproductive effort. This has a positive effect on our mind and body—as well as on our efficiency ratings.

Even more important, our increasing capacity to attend to internal events significantly increases our perceptual awareness, for by reducing extraneous thoughts we become free to attend to the great wealth of perceptual data that usually goes by unnoticed (thoughts, feelings, sensory data, and physiological processes as well as external environmental events). Normally we utilize only a small amount of this information simply because we do not allow it to come into conscious awareness. If we increase our ability to attend to perceptual data, however, we will find that we have increasingly greater control over the physical and mental processes involved with stress—and meditation is the only process by which one can systematically increase this awareness. As a matter of fact, this is the essence of the meditative process.

Remember that stress is primarily the result of a perceived threat to the self (or sense of I-ness). This includes anything that we identify with the sense of self or anything that we are emotionally involved with or attached to. It is this very personal sense of I-ness that undergoes a gradual evolutionary transformation through the process of meditation. This does not come about suddenly. It is, rather, the result of one's developing internal awareness that there is a center of consciousness (a transpersonal self) which is distinct from both mind and body—and not affected by change. As this self evolves, it becomes a center of unshakable tranquility and allows one to remain calm in the face of adversity—and slowly one begins to identify with it.

We recognize that change is the stimulus to fear and stress. So when one has the ability to view all change—no matter how personal and intimate or sudden or drastic—with calmness and detachment, one's ability to deal adequately with it is dramatically increased. Thus, the only practical response to the dissipation, turmoil and disruption in this world of "future shock" is for each of us to experience this personal center of tranquility.

The transpersonal self cannot be experience through therapy, drugs, reading books or having wonderful parents. It cannot be experienced through intellectual discourse or by going to college. It is already deep within our minds, but it can be experienced only by allowing inner concentration to evolve into meditation. This leads to the superconscious self. This experience is characterized by pure consciousness (or awareness without any object), tranquility and an innate sense of inner joy and peace. It is accompanied by absolute mastery over our emotional states.

During the process of establishing our new identity with this superconscious self, we slowly disidentify with those aspects of ourselves which we considered for so long to be essential to our sense of identity—our thoughts and ideas, our emotions, our body and behaviors, our roles and social attachments. In short, as we develop our skills in concentration and meditation, we slowly begin to put our old self into a new and more useful perspective. And as we gain emotional distance, we increase our ability to perceive our former "identity" with greater clarity. We thus become less reactive to stressful situations and have greater conscious control over our actions.

This process will be more clear if we can understand the evolutionary growth that is a part of the meditative process. Maturity is measured, in a sense, by our ability to grow out of our self-imposed limitations. Thus, as our experience and understanding increase, and as we give up our past identities, we slowly become aware of our greater and greater potential for freedom and self-control. And we naturally disassociate with those past identities that are based on a more limited (and more limiting) awareness. How much more practical can you be than that!

This has been just a brief overview of the process of inner concentration and meditation; it is intended only to give you a practical understanding of the importance of training the mind and expanding one's conscious awareness. It involves self-training, and as with any training program, it takes time and practice. The rewards, however, are far greater than the effort involved. Almost immediately you will begin to experience increased mental and physical health, increased mental clarity and control, increased personal effectiveness—and most important, an increased capacity for experiencing joy. The more skillful you become, the greater the rewards.

Exercises are provided in this book so that you can begin practicing inner concentration. They are included so that you may have something concrete to work with, and they are effective. If you practice them systematically, you will gain control over your levels of stress. However—do yourself a favor. Seek out a competent teacher and learn the basics of meditation, for a good teacher can point out the pitfalls and provide the fundamental skills and tools. He can help refine the process. Remember, though, that your goal is independence and freedom. The teacher cannot do your meditation for you, and he cannot eliminate your stress for you. Only you can do that.

It is our heritage to be healthy—physically, mentally and spiritually. Meditation is the tool by which we become aware of the habits which have disrupted, altered and interfered with that heritage. Increased awareness is the process which leads to freedom from these habits. If you want to do this, the tools are available. The choices are up to you.

Summaries and Beginnings

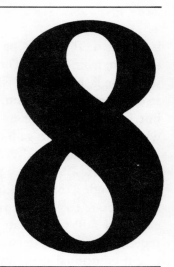

Stress is a "blind" condition of the mind that is far more injurious than any other. As we have seen, however, it need not be a permanent feature of our lives, for we can begin to take charge of ourselves in such a way as to maintain physical, mental and spiritual balance. We can use our time and energy to fulfill our potential rather than wasting it on fatigue, anxiety, disease and other mental and physical disturbances.

The word *personality* comes from the root *persona*, a Greek word meaning mask. Our personality is a mask that is woven by our character—which is composed of our habits. Once a habit is formed, however, it can become a deeply grooved channel and cause habitual stress. When we think of becoming free of stress, we should carefully examine our habit patterns. We can transform the whole personality by training ourselves, by allowing our mind to create new grooves. Thus, it will modify itself, and once this has happened the character is changed, the habit patterns are changed and we can get freedom from stress. This is possible if we work with ourselves on a holistic basis. Simply focusing on one aspect of stress, such as relaxation, will give us some relief, it is true— but it will never give us the self-awareness and self-control which is required to gain complete freedom.

Freedom is really the knowledge and ability to choose our responses. Stress is a prison built by our emotional habits and attitudes towards life; it is sustained by our ignorance. So if we are to gain our freedom we must develop the knowledge and skill to regulate our own internal realities. To do so requires that we understand and regulate the internal sources of our emotional structures.

The Four Primitive Urges

Yoga science points out that there are four instinctual urges, or primitive drives, which are inherent in our biological structure: self-preservation, food, sleep and sex. They exist in both animals and man, and they serve to insure both the survival of the individual and the continuation of the species. These drives lead us to protect ourselves from danger, to seek out food for nourishment, to give ourselves adequate rest for revitalization, and to participate in the creation of new life so that the species may continue. They are the source of energy for our emotions, but they are not the emotions themselves. In other words, they are, as it were, unfocused or undirected fountains of energy which supply power to the emotions. Desires are the channeling of these basic urges into a specific object or experience in order to satisfy the underlying urge or drive. Thus man can, and has, created an almost endless number of desires, for there are a great number of objects that can satisfy the basic urges.

It is at the level of desire that we set the conditions for our emotions. If the object satisfies the urge, the particular desire (together with its connection to that object) is reinforced, and thus strengthened. It is as if the desire is a channel which is deepened if the chosen object satisfies the desire, and every time this happens the probability is increased that this particular channel (desire to object) will be utilized again. Soon the connection between the desire and the object becomes so strong that the desire and the object come to be seen as one and the same. In other words, there is now a deep groove that leads immediately to the object for the expression of the urge. Neither the basic urge nor the desire, however, are emotions. Figure 1 shows how the conversion takes place.

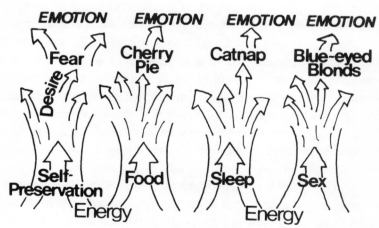

Figure 1
THE RELATIONSHIP BETWEEN THE PRIMITIVE DRIVES, DESIRES AND EMOTIONS

To begin with, energy flows through the four fountains (primitive urges). As the flow takes a specific direction toward an object, it becomes known as desire. Then, from the interaction and connection of the desire and the object of desire, emotions are created. For example we have an urge for food. While there may be plenty available, we are "hungry" for a particular dish—cherry pie. Hunger, the urge, is now directed to a particular object; we desire the cherry pie even though it may not provide nourishment, the sole reason for the hunger.

As the channel becomes deeper (as the relationship between the desire and the object becomes stronger) we become more and more attached to the object. In time we become dependent upon it in order to satisfy the desire. At this point a very strong habit has been conditioned into our personality at the level of desire. In other words, it is the dependency upon the object of desire that leads to an emotion. As is so clearly stated by Swami Rama and Swami Ajaya in *Emotion to Enlightenment*, "It is in seeking to obtain and keep objects of our desire that we become emotional in one way or another. Thus it is said that desire is the mother of all emotions." Emotional imbalance, in fact, always involves one's relationships to the external world. Not a single emotion has an exclusively internal source; they always arise from one's relationship to some desired object or person.

This principle also operates when there is displeasure, or pain, and we develop a habit of aversion rather than attraction. Instead of desiring to go to a particular object or experience, we desire to avoid it.

The emotions that create problems for us, the negative

emotions, arise when the desire is unfulfilled, or blocked, or somehow threatened. For example, when someone or something prevents us from obtaining our desire, or threatens to take away an object of our desire, we become angry. This, in turn, upsets our balance—and we suffer from stress. Even though we may express our anger, thus relieving some measure of stress, the damage (internal imbalance) has already begun. The best we can do now is to eliminate the anger as quickly as possible.

Fear, another negative emotion, is an outgrowth of the urge for self-preservation, and it is a major source of stress. We experience fear when we feel that our existence, or our sense of self-worth or completeness, depends upon an external object and we anticipate the loss of that object or the inability to gain what we think we need. As the authors of *Emotion to Enlightenment* point out, "Without the habit of dependency there could be no fear." Other negative emotions are jealousy (or envy), greed, depression and pride,* and all of them are related to an attachment, or identification, with the objects of our desires. They arise when this dependency is somehow threatened or interfered with. These emotions are subject to conditioning through pleasure and pain, and thus they can form very strong habits.

Disturbances can also be created as a consequence of fulfilling desires. For example, eating the cherry pie will satisfy the desire, but it also creates a disturbance because the pie is loaded with refined sugar. This leads to an imbalance in the digestive process, and this in turn leads to stress. Greed,

---

* For a more complete description of this subject see Swami Rama and Swami Ajaya, *Emotion to Enlightenment* (Honesdale: The Himalayan Institute, 1976).

another negative emotion, arises when we already possess the objects of our desire but this possession only feeds the desire further. In fact, one of the main difficulties that we must recognize is that through fulfilling desire, we set the stage for it to be active again in the future. Thus, we must become sensitive to the consequences of our desires.

Modern psychology focuses on the emotions, but they are not the true source of our difficulties. It is the four basic urges, the source of our emotional energy, that must be regulated if we are to become free from stress. To do this we must begin to discriminate between the emotion (such as anger or fear) and the emotional power behind it. In other words, it is through controlling and regulating the emotional power (the primitive urge) that one can become free from stress. This power can be channeled either destructively or constructively. If the emotional flow is channeled destructively, we suffer the negative emotions and related diseases. If it is channeled constructively, it can flow smoothly, satisfying the primitive urges and leading to healthy creative living.

We can regulate the four primitive urges by regulating their expression. For example, the urge for self-preservation is not limited to protecting one's physical existence; it extends to anything that becomes emotionally important or involved with our sense-of-I-ness. This includes our personality, our body, job, family or social position. When unregulated, this urge can express itself in ego trips and selfishness, for we attach importance to all sorts of people, objects and experiences in order to feel secure, important, fulfilled, or happy. Then we come to depend upon these external objects for our happiness, and the world becomes filled with fear if they are threatened. (If you think about it closely, you will see that selfishness, the need to enhance the ego, is directly related to fear.) Through meditation, however, and the practice of "self-less-ness," we learn that our happiness resides within—and as we increase our inner security we are able to release our dependency on external objects. Thus, no matter how things come and go in the external world, we remain secure and balanced.

The primitive urge for food must also be regulated and controlled. As we have seen in chapter five, disturbances in our digestive system lead to disturbances in many other functions. By regulating the "what, when and how" of food intake we can satisfy this primitive urge by taking nutritionally useful food at proper times and in a proper way. Thus, difficulties that are related to food intake (such as compulsive eating, indigestion and obesity) as well as the associated emotional disturbances (such as guilt, fear and self-hatred) are brought under control. Practicing good dietary habits will also lead to the desire for healthy food, thus channeling this urge constructively.

We should also practice good sleeping habits. Most people have disturbed sleep, and this, too, underlies stress. It is obvious to all when we "get out of bed on the wrong side" or when we experience the disturbances that result from insomnia. In addition, sleep is very subtly connected with our emotions. Our dreams, for instance, not only reflect our unconscious desires and emotions, they actually strengthen them. Furthermore, disturbed sleep interferes with the necessary revitalization process and prevents the body from achieving full benefit from the rest. Thus it is important that we begin to study and regulate the unconscious activity that takes place in sleep.

You can do this only if you regulate your sleeping habits and train yourself to sleep properly. Diet, exercise, breathing exercises and meditation are the means. The sleep exercise (given in chapter six), for instance, quiets the unconscious and allows for deep and peaceful sleep as well as regulates its very nature. Then you will find that the time spent sleeping decreases while the quality of the sleep increases. In this way sleep becomes truly revitalizing—an important element in developing freedom from stress.

The fourth and final primitive urge, sex, is different from the other three. For one thing, it is not necessary for our personal survival. More important, since it is extremely pleasurable it fosters strong attachments. In addition, since it involves another person's needs and moods, its full expression is unpredictable. Therefore the area of sex is extremely fertile ground for the development of negative emotions such as jealousy, greed, anger and fear. Any therapist will tell you that sexual conflicts are by far the most prevalent emotional disturbance in modern society.

Self-regulation of this urge requires that one regulate both the mental and physical aspects of sexual activity—and this can be accomplished through voluntarily limiting the frequency of the act and by developing a stable partnership. That is not based on some moral view; it is the practical recognition that desire is strengthened by every repeated act as well as by increasing the number of objects of desire. Anxiety is then generated by the fact that the outcome (whether or not one will possess the object of desire) is unpredictable. Thus, to gain control over the powerful sexual urge one must consciously fix the time and place for sexual expression with a chosen partner. Then, as one begins to alter his attachments to previous patterns of behavior, his control over the expression of this energy flow also increases.

Hatha yoga exercises help redirect this flow away from troublesome desires toward a more general expression in physical activity and involvement in the world around us. At the same time, breathing exercises and meditation help maintain a calm mind and allow for increased self-awareness. These all help in developing control. The sexual urge then becomes an extremely important ally in creative work, loving relationships and expanded levels of consciousness.

Thus, self-regulation of the four primitive urges is necessary if we are to use our emotional power creatively and be free from disease. Regulation does not mean suppressing or repressing—this will lead to a negative emotional state and imbalance. Self-regulation means the conscious channeling of the energy flow into appropriate uses and objects; it means withdrawing our dependency upon the objects of our desires.

Self-regulation requires self-awareness, and self-awareness requires self-regulation. Neither can be successful without the other. Self-awareness without self-regulation degenerates into selfishness and is characterized by self-indulgence and a limiting of personality and growth. Self-regulation without self-awareness results in a rigid fanaticism that leads to increased suppression and repression as well as destructive emotional outbursts. If we combine the two, however, then we can begin to free ourselves from the habits that we developed in our ignorance, habits that nearly always lead to stress. Gradually then, we begin to lose our dependency upon the objects of our desires and thus eliminate the power of negative emotions that create imbalance.

Not all desires, however, spring from the four urges,

nor are all emotions negative. Yoga science points to another desire which does not stem from the primitive urges—the desire for higher knowledge. This has its roots in the spiritual nature of man. It is what leads him to explore both the external universe and the internal truth, and it can be so powerful that even the primitive urges will come under its control.

This desire for higher knowledge leads to the positive emotions of love, joy and peace. The tool of love is selflessness, for we are not speaking of the love one feels toward someone who has satisfied one's needs. It is actually the opposite; this love is an expansion of oneself, an outward flow marked by selflessness in action, speech and thought. It seeks no reward or return, which shows that it is free from attachment and dependency. The more one practices selflessness in daily life, the more freedom one gains.

Joy, the second positive emotion, is what we experience when we love, and it is necessary for maintaining inner and outer harmony in life. Laughter, the tool of joy, is probably one of the best techniques for stress management that is available to man; joy, as it expresses itself in laughter, is the light that illumines our path through life. Joy is cultivated through seeking another's happiness; it is never found when we are seeking our own. It is also found in the experience of being oneself without pretense or apology. Thus the practice of self-awareness (and its twin, self-regulation) brings about the experience of joy, and those who are truly joyful are free from suffering.

The last positive emotion, peace, is the expression of complete acceptance of oneself. This is not passivity or apathy; it is rather, a state of tranquility that signifies a balanced mind. Then one is not disturbed by the turns and tumbles of the events and objects of the world, yet one is able to fully enjoy and use these events and objects. This peace is not characterized by withdrawal from the world, but by complete and skillful participation in it. It is a peaceful mind that comprehends the absolute fullness of life and can participate in it. Meditation is the tool of peace.

This desire for higher knowledge, and its accompanying positive emotions, are thus very powerful aids in becoming free from stress, for in the last analysis we are the source of our own suffering. Consequently, it is we who must eliminate it. Only we have the power to alter those habits of behaving, perceiving and feeling that result in stress. They were not acquired overnight, nor will they be magically altered overnight. Freedom from stress is the consequence of skillful living, and just as any skill development takes time and training, learning to live skillfully requires patient self-training.

Self-Training: Pathway to Knowledge

There are two broad categories of training external training and self-training. The first is externally imposed discipline based on the suggestions and information we receive from others. This training builds habits, but it does not allow one to build these habits on the basis of direct inner experience and one's evaluation of this experience. Consequently, it leads to an "ignorant," or "blind," mind, for it does not require that we fully understand what we are learning. In external training one is asked only to accept, believe, and/or behave in a certain way. No matter how beneficial the intent, external training leads to a constriction of awareness, dependency and inner conflict.

We may gain information through external training, and we may form habits because of it—but if these are not based on direct experiential knowledge, then one is not truly confident. And without self-confidence one is indecisive. Indecision leads to conflict and stress. Then, when our mind is divided and our habits are in conflict we end up doing what we really don't want to be doing and rarely do what we want to do. This makes for inner conflict which divides our will—and we are unable to remain in balance. Another way of saying this is that while everyone wants to enjoy life, very few develop the capacity to do this. Our minds are too scattered, our awareness too limited by the suggestions we accept, and our will too weakened.

Self-training, on the other hand, is based on the expansion of one's awareness and the ability to guide or direct that awareness. In self-training one does not accept suggestion (someone else's experience) as the basis for decision. Instead, one seeks to discover his own inner reality through directing and examining his own experience. In this way one gains self-confidence and develops the power of will, the ability to discriminate, to decide and to carry through that decision in thought, speech and action. Self-training involves all aspects of one's life, from self-study and relaxation to regulation of the four primitive urges.

To give a concrete example of the two methods of training, there are two different approaches to teaching relaxation. External relaxation training utilizes suggestion and autosuggestion, generally in the form of imagery, to create a state of relaxation. This is the method usually used by psychologists, psychiatrists and other therapists—and is effective to a limited degree. Self-training however utilizes the corpse posture, diaphragmatic breathing and observation of a smooth, even flow of breath (without jerks, pauses, shallowness or noise). The awareness is directed towards what is taking place in the body, and this leads to expanded awareness and thus to greater control. One can easily tell the difference between relaxation based on suggestion and relaxation based on diaphragmatic breathing and direct awareness. The first leads only to a state of relaxation; the latter leads to a state of inner knowledge and balance—as well as a much deeper state of relaxation.

The purpose of self-training is to develop the self-confidence that comes from self-knowledge and self-control. This increases our capacity to consciously direct our mind, speech and actions, for when we no longer create inner conflicts through indecisiveness, we control and direct the flow of emotional energy and achieve balance. The mind that is free from stress is a tranquil mind, and this is the basis for success in life—for if one has a tranquil mind, the energy which was consumed by stress can now be used to gain deeper knowledge and develop our creative abilities.

There is still one area to examine if we are to develop complete freedom from stress, and that is our attitudes, for they play a major role in our day-to-day life. Positive attitudes are essential prerequisites for good health, while negative and passive attitudes are the source of many psychosomatic diseases. There are three positive attitudes which seem to be essential to self-training. In fact, there are very probably more than three (and you can add as many as you wish), but they should not be taken as moral absolutes. They are practical guides.

Self-Responsibility

First you must recognize that you are solely responsible for yourself and your own world. That does not mean either that you have created the world or that the world is a figment of your imagination. It means that you are the one who defines and assigns to yourself, whether consciously or unconsciously, the meaning of the world, its events, objects and people. What you are accepting is the responsibility for your own internal events—your thoughts, feelings, physiological processes and behavior.

The necessity for taking this responsibility becomes more clear when we examine the nature of our perceptual processes. Remember that in the third chapter we discussed how we organize all incoming sensory data into categories. What we then relate to is not the raw sensory data, but rather the organization of that data. We might compare this organizing facility of the mind to a large filtering mechanism. Figure 2 below gives a simplified illustration of this process. As you can see, input from the external world is taken through the sensory faculties into the organizing faculty where it is grouped into meaningful categories, concepts and relationships. In addition, there is evidence to show that we even program our senses to select out data from the external world. Thus, the raw data is brought into the filter, organized and then presented to the sense of "I-ness," or personality, and to the discriminating faculty. Only then do we relate to it and decide what to do with it.

No matter how much we study the outside world, if we do not know what the filtering mechanism does, then there is no way we will be able to understand our reactions

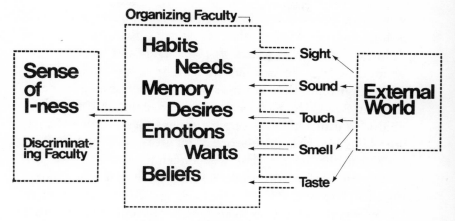

Figure 2
**CATEGORIES AND CONCEPTS SHAPED BY THE
CONTENTS OF THE MIND**

to the world. In other words, only by accepting the fact that we organize our own minds and then beginning to study the filter mechanism directly (through inner concentration and meditation), can we hope to truly undertand why we behave, think and feel the way we do. As long as we avoid this responsibility, blaming others (or events) for how we feel, think and behave, we can never gain the necessary knowledge of (and control over) those habits and patterns which result in stress, fear and disease.

Self-Acceptance

Self-acceptance does not mean a pat-on-the back—"I'm O.K. no matter what" attitude, nor is it self-serving egotism. True self-acceptance is the ability to look clearly at all aspects of yourself and to recognize their fundamental unity. Self-acceptance is also the recognition that mistakes and failures are opportunities for learning and growth, not whipping-sticks for self-punishment. It is also the practical realization that one's intrinsic value is never altered by petty stupidities. As human beings, we all commit errors. The ability to utilize them as opportunities to learn rather than as stumbling blocks is the essence of maturity.

To the degree that we condemn ourselves, we will create unnecessary suffering. To the degree that we condemn ourselves, we will also condemn others. Self-acceptance leads to acceptance of others. The biblical commandment, "love thy neighbor as thyself" is on one level an accurate description of reality. That is, you can only love others to the extent that you can love yourself. This does not mean that you have an egotistical and selfish concern for your personality; it means that you have a deep and abiding respect for the universal consciousness that is inherent in all of us.

Both self-acceptance and self-responsibility are extremely practical. For instance, most of us focus on only part of the truth about ourselves. That is, we tend to see only that part of ourselves which satisfies our emotional need or condition at a given time. It's very easy to focus on negativity when one is feeling depressed, or "down on himself," for example. Then all we can see are our mistakes, our petty faults and stupidities. Of course the consequence of this "inner concentration" is continued suffering and depression. Or perhaps we do something marvelously well, and we become big-headed in our egotism. Either attitude is based on a partial understanding, an incomplete awareness of the truth about ourselves.

To gain full awareness of our inner realities requires that we begin to look at ourselves in a calm, detached way, to observe our personality, the workings of our mind and body, from a neutral viewpoint. We thus sharpen our faculty of discrimination, our ability to see clearly the relationship between cause and effect, without judgment.

You might ask, "Why without judgment?" The answer is that judgment implies a right or wrong, good or bad value placed upon the cause-effect relationship, and this leads to emotional involvement. But to understand our inner workings clearly, we must be able to experience them directly without interference from our emotions and defense mechanisms. This enables us to alter the inner processes which we decide are not helpful. If judgment is used instead of discrimination, the direct experiential knowledge of the subtle cause/effect relationships of the mind will be obscured by our emotional attachment to a "good" or "bad" outcome. It is very probable that our judgments would then be wrong, as they would be based on inaccurate information.

Self-acceptance, on the other hand, allows one to come to know, to experience directly, the truth about oneself. The very practical consequence of this knowledge has been stated in many ways, and for thousands of years. In the Western world it is reflected in the biblical statement, "The truth shall set you free." In the Eastern world it is reflected in the Vedantic statement, "Knowledge is that which liberates."

Skeptical Curiosity

In learning about yourself one of the most helpful attitudes is that of skeptical curiosity. Obviously, curiosity is necessary, but if it feeds only a superficial analysis, then your ability to discriminate, to observe your mind with detachment and dispassion, is greatly impeded. There is need for a little skepticism about whatever answers your mind presents to you. Remembering that your purpose is not to find answers, but only to observe, will help the natural evolutionary process of inner transformation and growth. But direct, experiential knowledge does not require that your mind analyze itself; it requires only that you become aware of what the mind is doing at the time it is doing it. You should be free from preconceived notions about what should be.

These three attitudes—self-responsibility, self-acceptance and skeptical curiosity—are integral to gaining freedom from stress. Fortunately, they are further developed and strengthened by the practice of meditation. So while they greatly help in your self-training program, the techniques of the self-training in turn strengthen the attitudes.

The First Step

Now that you have the basic information, you can establish your own self-training program. For in the last analysis, the process of gaining freedom from stress requires that you actually do the necessary breathing, relaxation and physical exercises as well as practice concentration and meditation. The whole person needs to be trained, not just an isolated part of the person. To this end there are a few points that you should keep in mind when establishing your own program:

1. *Begin with the practice of diaphragmatic breathing.* Proper regulation of the breath is of primary importance in

stress management. In fact, diaphragmatic breathing must take place if one is to eliminate unnecessary levels of arousal in the body. If your breathing rate is "normal," (if it is between sixteen and twenty breaths per minute), you can be fairly sure that you are suffering from stress.

A minimum practice is to concentrate on breathing from your diaphragm for five to ten minutes, three times a day. This will lead to the reestablishment of diaphragmatic breathing as your habitual pattern. It will also do much to reduce the accumulated stress in the body, and begin to prepare the mind for concentration exercises.

2. *Begin your self-training program very gently.* Don't expect yourself to start an all-out program, spending an hour or two every day on it. You will tire of this superficial discipline very quickly—and quickly decide to stop doing anything. The most successful programs are those that are built slowly and methodically. Decide what you can do on a daily basis that will not interfere with your essential duties. Then make sure that you practice according to that schedule every day.

When one exercise, or period of practice, has become habitual (a regular part of your daily routine) then add on to that practice. For example, once you have become accustomed to spending five or ten minutes on diaphragmatic breathing every morning, add five minutes of concentration on breath awareness (concentrating on the feeling of the breath at the opening of the nostrils). Then slowly expand that period of concentration to your capacity. If there are times when you feel that you can't concentrate, simply practice your breathing, but do not do something else with the time you have set aside for practice.

This same method of scheduling should be applied to your physical exercise. If you do five minutes of stretching, slowly expand the time and the amount you exercise—after the first five minutes has become routine. Self-discipline is a matter of slowly acquiring the habits you want to have. It should not be self-punishment. Avoid sudden and dramatic changes, as this will most often lead to resistance and problems. Study yourself; learn to understand your needs, and gradually shape your behavior to satisfy those needs in a systematic and regulated way.

3. *Be consistent.* Even if you do only five minutes of diaphragmatic breathing daily, do that every day. Consistent practice develops skill. The more systematic you are, the greater will be your progress. It definitely helps if you set aside a specific time every day in which to practice. This establishes the habit. You will also find that this daily time period in itself will become a stimulus for inducing a state of relaxation and calm. The same is true if you select a certain room or place to do your practice in, for it will become associated with relaxation and further reinforce your practice. In this vein, it is important that the place be quiet, clean and well ventilated. Don't expect to gain skill in inner concentration and relaxation by practicing in the corporate cafeteria.

4. *Work within your own capacity.* Your goal is increased awareness, not a particular state or exercise. Learn to let your concentration flow; it should not be forced (forced relaxation or concentration only creates tension). If you are trying to beat the clock or set some kind of record,

you will only create more tension. Remember that you are only trying to discover the truth about yourself right now, at this moment; you are not trying to become an expert at anything. By working consistently and systematically within your own unique capacity, you will definitely expand that capacity.

5. *Be patient.* Allow time for progress to take place. Be gentle with yourself; trust in your innate capacity for growth. Trees, flowers, plants and animals all grow to fulfill their innate potential. You have that same capacity. Tension is produced when you try to structure yourself instead of allowing your innate capacity to unfold in its own natural, inevitable way. So learn to trust yourself. This will help you grow, and at the same time you will create a minimum of stress. Above all, understand that your program is to be very practical. Each time that you practice, it is an excursion into awareness and tranquility—so enjoy what you are doing fully. In this way you will learn to enjoy the objects of the world as well, but you will not be lost in dependency.

A Possible Program

Below is a possible self-training program. It is just an outline to guide you, for you must establish your own unique program based on your own schedule, needs and goals. Each of us will find different techniques more suitable to us than others and different times for practice more convenient. Generally, early morning is best for concentration practice. Your body is rested and your mind is fairly refreshed then, not humming with the day's activities. Experiment with

TABLE 1
SUGGESTED DAILY SCHEDULE
FOR RELAXATION / MEDITATION TECHNIQUES

Morning:
> 5 minutes diaphragmatic breathing (this can be done immediately upon awakening).
> Shower or bath: loosens up the muscles, clears the mind.
> 5 minutes of stretching exercises.
> 5-10 solar salutations: begin with 2 or 3, gradually increasing the number over a period of weeks until doing 12 or more.
> 10 minutes of breath awareness: gradually increase to 20 minutes.

During the Day:
> 5 minutes of 2:1 ratio diaphragmatic breathing.
> Breath awareness as often as you can.
> Take a 10 minute relaxation break in the morning and afternoon; you will be surprised at how it helps clarify your thinking.

After Work:
> Relaxation exercise: this is an excellent time to clear your mind of work-related tensions.
> Breath awareness: 10 minutes, gradually increase to 15 or 20 minutes.

Evening:
> 5 minutes of 2:1 ratio diaphragmatic breathing (can be done in bed right before going to sleep).
> Breath awareness: this concentration should be done at least once daily. 20 minutes of concentration on the breath is worth 60 minutes of relaxation exercises.

Using the breath awareness technique as often as you can during the day will gradually increase your ability to stay calm and relaxed.

This schedule is only a guide. Evolve your own schedule and slowly increase the time spent on concentration/meditation exercises. The key is to be consistent!

yourself. Don't be afraid to try a technique for a month and see what the consequences are. The more sophisticated the technique, the deeper and more subtle will be the changes.

It is strongly recommended that you work with a competent meditation teacher, preferably one who has had years of training in breathing and meditation techniques. While this book gives you sufficient information to begin your practice, meditation itself should be learned directly from a good teacher. When selecting one, examine both his training and experience as well as his students (the biblical phrase, "By their fruits shall ye know them" definitely applies in this situation). The teacher should also be inspiring and should exhibit some degree of self-awareness and self-control.

Beyond Stress Management

Among the various sources of stress, fear seems to be the greatest. It is a "will-killer" that cripples us and prevents us from becoming creative, thus destroying our human potential. When we begin to objectively examine our fears, however, we begin to discover an untapped capacity for life that we had only vague notions and dreams of before. Just as the calm depths of a lake lie hidden beneath its turbulent surface, so does our true potential lie hidden by the sound and fury of our fears.

It is not by accident that the same tools which eliminate fears also lead us to experience, directly and consciously, our true selves. For freedom from stress is, in a very real sense, freedom from fear. This has been known to yoga for thousands of years. So by beginning to regulate your breath and develop your powers of inner concentration and meditation, you have taken the first steps on a journey which can lead to the fullest utilization of your inner potential. Each step, however small, leads to greater understanding and to an increased capacity for living life in all its fullness and richness. In other words, our fears cause us to be only partly human. To become fully human is to discover the peace within and to live using our full capacity.

Do not be content with just a little relaxation or a healthier coronary-vascular system. These you can have—and much, much more. Experience your true nature directly. Calm the body; then calm the mind through self-training. Allow no movement of body or mind to disturb the clarity of your inner perception. Meditation will lead you to fulfill the most meaningful question of all—"Who am I?"

It is important to remember again, however, that we are talking about meditation—not religious ritual. They should not be confused. Meditation is a practical technique for understanding human nature at all levels, and this is the most important thing one can do. The great sages of all cultures have been very practical men and women who, through meditation, have sought for and discovered genuine and lasting release from fear and suffering. What they discovered may be found in many languages, in many religions, in many cultures. It is found in Sophocles' statement, "Know Thyself"; it is "Be still and know that I am God" in the Jewish tradition; it is "The kingdom of God is within" in the Christian tradition; and in the Vedantic tradition it is "That I am." Every culture expresses this one great truth in some way.

This, then, is our heritage. This, then, can be our achievement. Nothing is more practical than to be free from fear. Nothing is more powerful than the direct and joyful experience of the inner self—and to discover that it has always been there. As T. S. Eliot said at the end of his last and greatest work, *The Four Quartets:*

> We shall not cease from exploration
> And the end of all our exploring
> Will be to arrive where we started
> And know the place for the first time.

Bibliography
of
Suggested Readings

Ajaya, Swami. *Yoga Psychology*. Honesdale, PA: The Himalayan Institute, 1976.

Arya, Usharbudh. *Philosophy of Hatha Yoga*. Honesdale, PA: The Himalayan Institute, 1977.

Averill, J., E. Olbrich and R. Lazarus. "Personality Correlates of Differential Responsiveness to Direct and Vicarious Threats." *Journal of Personality and Social Psychology*, 1972, 25-29.

———— *Superconscious Meditation*. Honesdale, PA: The Himalayan Institute, 1978.

Ballentine, Rudolph. *Diet and Nutrition*. Honesdale, PA: The Himalayan Institute, 1978.

Barber, T. V. *LSD, Marihuana, Yoga and Hypnosis*. Chicago: Aldine, 1971.

Benson, Herbert. *The Relaxation Response*. New York: Avon Books, 1976.

Brown, Barbara. *Supermind*. New York: Harper and Row, 1980.

———— *Stress and the Art of Biofeedback*. New York: Harper and Row, 1977.

Clarke, John. "Characterization of the Resting Breath Pattern." *Research Bulletin of the Himalayan International Institute*, Fall, 1979, 7-9.

Cottle, Maurice. "Rhinomanometry: Clinical Application in Family and Rhinologic Practice." *Seminar Manual: American Rhinologic Society*, 1980.

Davidson, Richard J. and Gary E. Schwartz. "The Psychology of Relaxation and Relaxed States: A Multi-process Theory," in *Behavior Control and Modifications of Physiological Activity*. Englewood Cliffs: Prentice-Hall, 1976, pp. 339-442.

Dychtwald, Ken. *Bodymind*. New York: Pantheon Books, 1977.

Eccles, John C. *Facing Reality*. New York: Springer-Verlag New York, 1975.

"Emotional Stress: Proceedings of the National Conference on Emotional

Stress and Heart Disease." *The Journal of the South Carolina Medical Association*, 72, No. 2 (February 1976).

Friedman, Meyer and Ray H. Rosenman. *Type A Behavior and Your Heart*. Greenwich: Fawcett, 1974.

Funderburk, James. *Science Studies Yoga*. Honesdale, PA: The Himalayan Institute, 1977.

Galway, W. Timothy. *The Inner Game of Tennis*. New York: Random House, 1974.

Gellhorn, E. and W. F. Kiely. "Mystical States of Consciousness: Neurophysical and Clinical Aspects." *Journal of Nervous and Mental Diseases*. 154 (1972), 399-405.

Green, Elmer, Alyce Green and E. Dale Walters. "Voluntary Control of Internal States: Psychological and Physiological." *Journal of Transpersonal Psychology* II-1 (1970), 1-26.

"Health Costs—What Limit?" *Time*, 28 May, 1979, pp. 60-68.

Holmes, Thomas H. and T. Stephenson Holmes. *How Change Can Make Us Ill*. Chicago: Blue Cross Association, 1974.

Hymes, Alan and Phil Nuernberger. "Breathing Patterns Found in Heart Attack Patients." *Research Bulletin of the Himalayan International Institute*, 2-2 (1980), 10-12.

Illich, Ivan. *Medical Nemesis*. New York: Pantheon Books, 1976.

Joints and Glands Exercises. Ed. Rudolph Ballentine. Honesdale, PA: Himalayan Institute, 1978.

Kobasa, S.C. "Stressful Life Events, Personality and Health: An Inquiry into Hardiness." *Journal of Personality and Social Psychology*, 1979, 1-11.

Maslow, Abraham. *The Further Reaches of Human Nature*. New York: The Viking Press, 1971.

————— *Toward a Psychology of Being*. New York: Van Nostrand, 1962.

Meditational Therapy. Ed. Swami Ajaya. Honesdale, PA: Himalayan Institute, 1977.

Merrill-Wolff, Franklin. *Pathways Through to Space*. New York: The Julian Press, 1973.

————— *Philosophy of Consciousness without an Object*. New York: The Julian Press, 1973.

Nuernberger, E.P., "The Use of Meditation in the Treatment of Alcoholism." Unpublished Doctoral Dissertation. University of Minnesota, 1977.

Patel, Chandra. "Twelve-Month Follow-up of Yoga and Biofeedback in the Management of Hypertension." *Lancet*, 62 (1975), ii.

————— "Yoga and Biofeedback in the Management of Stress in Hypertensive Patients." *Clinical Science and Molecular Medicine*, 48 (1975), 171s-174s.

Patel, Chandra and M. Carruthers. "Coronary Risk Factor Reduction through Biofeedback-Aided Relaxation and Meditation." *Journal of the Royal College of General Practitioners*, 27 (1977), 401-405.

Penfield, Wilder. *The Mystery of the Mind*. Princeton: Princeton University Press, 1975.

Pelletier, Kenneth R. *Mind as Healer, Mind as Slayer*. New York: Delta, 1977.

Physicians Desk Reference. Ed. Emily Brogeler et al. Gradell, NJ: Litton, 1970.

Popper, Karl and John Eccles. *The Self and Its Brain*. New York: Springer-Verlag New York, 1977.

Price, Weston. *Nutrition and Physical Degeneration*. La Mesa, CA: Price-Pottinger Foundation, 1972.

Rahe, Richard H. "Stress and Strain in Coronary Heart Disease." *Emotional Stress: Proceedings of the National Conference on Emotional Stress and Heart Disease* in *Journal of the South Carolina Medical Association*, 72-2 (February 1976).

Rama, Swami. *A Practical Guide to Holistic Health*. Honesdale, PA: The Himalayan Institute, 1980.

———— *Lectures on Yoga*. Honesdale, PA: The Himalayan Institute, 1979.

Rama, Swami, and Swami Ajaya. *Emotion to Enlightenment*. Honesdale, PA: The Himalayan Institute, 1976.

Rama, Swami, Rudolph Ballentine and Alan Hymes. *Science of Breath: A Practical Guide*. Honesdale, PA: The Himalayan Institute, 1979.

Rama, Swami, Rudolph Ballentine and Swami Ajaya. *Yoga and Psychotherapy*. Honesdale, PA: The Himalayan Institute, 1976.

Seligman, Martin E. P. *Helplessness: On Depression, Development and Death*. San Francisco: W. H. Freeman, 1975.

Samskrti and Veda. *Hatha Yoga Manual I*. Honesdale, PA: The Himalayan Institute, 1977.

Samskrti and Judith Franks. *Hatha Yoga Manual II*. Honesdale, PA: The Himalayan Institute, 1978.

Selye, Hans. *The Stress of Life*. New York: McGraw-Hill, 1976.

———— *Stress without Distress*. New York: J. B. Lippincott, 1974.

"The Sleep Apnea Syndrome." *Krock Foundation Series*. Ed. C. Guillemainault and W. C. Dement. New York: Alan R. Liss, Inc., 1978.

Toffler, Alvin. *Future Shock*. New York: Random House, 1970.

Udupa, K. N. *Disorders of Stress and their Management by Yoga*. Banaras: Banaras Hindu University Press, 1978.

Wallace, R. K. and Herbert Benson. "The Physiology of Meditation."

Scientific American, 266 (1972), 84-90.
Williams, Roger J. *Nutrition Against Disease.* New York: Bantam, 1973.

Index

The Author

Phil Nuernberger, Ph.D., was born in Illinois in 1942; he completed his Ph.D. in Counseling Psychology in 1977 at the University of Minnesota. His doctoral thesis was on the use of meditation in the treatment of alcoholism.

Since 1969 Dr. Nuernberger has been deeply involved in the study of the science of yoga and the mind/body relationship under the personal direction and guidance of his teacher, Sri Swami Rama. In 1972 he traveled to the Himalayan Mountains in India where he studied the science of yoga in all its aspects.

From 1975 to 1979 he was a Director of Biofeedback Therapy at the Minneapolis Clinic of Psychiatry and Neurology. He is now a director of the Himalayan Institute as well as a member of the permanent faculty.

A dynamic speaker, Dr. Nuernberger travels extensively, lecturing on stress management, holistic health and the psychology of the East and West. He also serves as a management consultant and conducts stress-management seminars for several large corporations. In addition, he was a contributing author to *Theory and Practice of Meditation, Psychology East and West* and *Meditational Therapy*.

The
Himalayan Institute

The Himalayan Institute was founded by Sri Swami Rama as a non-profit organization whose charter outlines the following goals: to teach meditational techniques for the personal growth of modern people and their society; to make known the harmonious view of world religions and philosophies; and to undertake scientific research for the benefit of humanity. This challenging task is met by people of all walks of life and all faiths who attend and participate in the courses and seminars. These continuous programs are designed for people of all ages in order that they may discover how to live more creatively. In the words of the founder, "By being aware of one's own potentials and abilities, one can become a perfect citizen, help the nation and serve humanity."

Located in Honesdale, Pennsylvania, the National Headquarters serves as the coordination center for all of the Institute activities across the country. Five buildings, on four hundred and twenty acres, house the various programs as well as research and publication facilities of the Institute.

The Institute staff includes physicians, scientists, psychologists, philosophers and university professors from various fields of learning. These professional men and women share a common involvement both as students themselves and as pioneers in realizing the aim of the Institute.

The Residential Program provides training in the basic yoga disciplines—diet, ethical behavior, hatha yoga and meditation. Students are also given guidance in a philosophy of living in a community environment.

Graduate Programs will offer the M.A. degree in three fields: Eastern Philosophy, Holistic Therapies, and Comparative Psychology and Psychotherapy. The school's environment and curricula provide an academic and practical synthesis of ancient and experiential Eastern traditions, and modern scientific traditions of the West.

Seminars and workshops are available throughout the year which provide intensive training and experience in such topics as Superconscious Meditation, hatha yoga, philosophy, psychology and various aspects of holistic health.

The Two-week Combined Therapy Program emphasizes a natural, holistic approach to physical and psychological problems. A comprehensive medical and nutritional evaluation is provided by staff physicians. The program includes daily consultations, individualized work with diet, biofeedback training, joints and glands exercises, relaxation techniques, training in various methods of breathing and meditation.

The Five-day Stress Management/Physical Fitness Program offers practical and individualized training which can be used to control the stress response. This includes biofeedback, relaxation skills, exercise, diet, breathing techniques and meditation.

A yearly International Congress, sponsored by the Institute, is devoted to the scientific and spiritual progress of modern man. Through lectures, workshops, seminars and practical demonstrations, it provides a forum for professionals and laymen to share their knowledge and research.

The Eleanor N. Dana Research Laboratory is the psychophysiological laboratory of the Institute which specializes in research on breathing, meditation and holistic therapies. Utilizing the full range of equipment for the measurement of respiration, stress, and relaxed states, the staff investigates Eastern teachings through studies based on Western experimental techniques.

A list of Himalayan Institute publications follows:

Living with the Himalayan Masters	Swami Rama
A Practical Guide to Holistic Health	Swami Rama
Freedom from the Bondage of Karma	Swami Rama
Book of Wisdom	Swami Rama
Lectures on Yoga	Swami Rama
Life Here and Hereafter	Swami Rama
Marriage, Parenthood and Enlightenment	Swami Rama
Emotion to Enlightenment	Swami Rama, Swami Ajaya
Science of Breath	Swami Rama, Rudolph Ballentine, M.D., Alan Hymes, M.D.
Yoga and Psychotherapy	Swami Rama, Rudolph Ballentine, M.D., Swami Ajaya
Superconscious Meditation	Usharbudh Arya, Ph.D.
Philosophy of Hatha Yoga	Usharbudh Arya, Ph.D.
Meditation and the Art of Dying	Usharbudh Arya, Ph.D.
God	Usharbudh Arya, Ph.D.
Yoga Psychology	Swami Ajaya
Foundations, Eastern/Western Psychology	Swami Ajay (ed)
Psychology East and West	Swami Ajaya (ed)
Meditational Therapy	Swami Ajaya (ed)
Diet and Nutrition	Rudolph Ballentine, M.D.

Joints and Glands Exercises	Rudolph Ballentine, M.D. (ed)
Yoga and Christianity	Justin O'Brien, Drs.
Freedom from Stress	Phil Nuernberger, Ph.D.
Science Studies Yoga	James Funderburk, Ph.D.
Homeopathic Remedies	Drs. Anderson, Buegel, Chernin
Hatha Yoga Manual I	Samskrti and Veda
Hatha Yoga Manual II	Samskrti and Judith Franks
Swami Rama of the Himalayas	L. K. Misra, Ph.D. (ed)
Philosophy of Death and Dying	M. V. Kamath
Practical Vedanta of Swami Rama Tirtha	Brandt Dayton (ed)
The Swami and Sam	Brandt Dayton
Sanskrit without Tears	S. N. Agnihotri, Ph.D.
Psychology of the Beatitudes	Arpita
Theory and Practice of Meditation	Himalayan Institute
Art and Science of Meditation	Himalayan Institute
Inner Paths	Himalayan Institute
Meditation in Christianity	Himalayan Institute
Faces of Meditation	Himalayan Institute
Therapeutic Value of Yoga	Himalayan Institute
Chants from Eternity	Himalayan Institute
Spiritual Diary	Himalayan Institute
Thought for the Day	Himalayan Institute
The Yoga Way Cookbook	Himalayan Institute
Himalayan Mountain Cookery	Martha Ballentine